SINK or SWIM

AN INSPIRING STORY OF COURAGE AND RESILIENCE AFTER BEING WIDOWED AT 36

AMY WILLIAMS

First published by Ultimate World Publishing 2021
Copyright © 2021 Amy Williams

ISBN

Paperback: 978-1-922497-78-9
Ebook: 978-1-922497-79-6

Amy Williams has asserted her rights under the Copyright, Designs and Patents Act 1988 to be identified as the author of this work. The information in this book is based on the author's experiences and opinions. The publisher specifically disclaims responsibility for any adverse consequences which may result from use of the information contained herein. Permission to use information has been sought by the author. Any breaches will be rectified in further editions of the book.

All rights reserved. No part of this publication may be reproduced, stored in or introduced into a retrieval system, or transmitted in any form, or by any means (electronic, mechanical, photocopying, recording or otherwise) without the prior written permission of the author. Any person who does any unauthorised act in relation to this publication may be liable to criminal prosecution and civil claims for damages. Enquiries should be made through the publisher.

Cover design: Ultimate World Publishing
Layout and typesetting: Ultimate World Publishing
Editor: Alex Floyd-Douglass
Author Photo: Ally Lombardo, GIGPIX PHOTOGRAPHY

Ultimate World Publishing
Diamond Creek,
Victoria Australia 3089
www.writeabook.com.au

"Amy's resilience and strength in the face of such grief is truly remarkable, and her story is one which will give hope and comfort to anyone who has faced the crushing weight the loss of a loved one brings. Her memoir is proof of the strength of the human spirit, and a timely reminder to us all in these uncertain times."

Elle Halliwell
Journalist and Speaker
Author of A Mother's Choice

About The Author

Amy was born in Perth, WA. She grew up in Kingsley; the northern suburbs, with her Mum, Dad and younger sister, Kate.

Amy attended *Lake Joondalup Baptist College* in *Joondalup* where she met her high school sweetheart and late-husband, Joe Williams. They were together from the age of 16 until he unexpectedly passed away at the young age of 36.

She and her three beautiful children, Henry, Ruby and Mia, live in their family home, in the northern coastal suburb of Wembley Downs.

In 2017, Amy received her *Diploma of Interior Design and Decoration* and started her own residential interior design business.

By 2020, Amy's heart was yearning for more; something deeper and more meaningful.

In her own process and years of grief, receiving counselling of various methods, discovering who she is as an individual, and having the sole care of three young children; two of whom have special needs, Amy has a lot of insight to share and inspire others.

With her growth mindset, positivity, strength, constant learning, understanding and growth in the field of grief and life challenges, Amy has been led to study Art Therapy. Her main interest lies in counselling young kids and teens going through grief, trauma and any difficulties in life, by using Art Therapy as a gentler approach.

Amy enjoys spending her time reading non-fiction and inspirational books, listening to music, learning spiritual and holistic practices, making soaps and natural body products, doing Pilates and Yin Yoga, going to the beach and catching up with friends and family.

Amy is creative, passionate, kind, gentle, loving and warm. She embraces life with open arms and spreads her positive vibes onto all those she meets.

About The Author

What People Are Saying About Amy

One of my favourite memories was visiting Joe and Amy in the UK, sightseeing in London for the day. They had been away from home for five years, so it was a sheer delight when Amy came home five months pregnant; I knew they were home to stay. I celebrated the birth of all three of their children. Ruby was born on Friday 18th December, U2 was playing at Subiaco Oval; Amy loved the *"free concert."* They were so happy. Amy had always been lucky; until the day she wasn't. Tuesday, 18th June 2013.

I didn't know how Amy would recover from such a tragedy. That depth of despair could have destroyed her spirit, her will to live. Would the love for her children be enough to raise her up to a state of wanting to make a new life?

Her seven-year journey has shown the hidden spirit that has always lived inside, only her inner and eternal searching has revealed the true spirit that is Amy Williams. Sink or Swim is her testimony to her genuinely positive outlook on a path to dealing with the worst of life's experiences.

Love you always.

Cliff Jackson
Dad

The hardest thing I've ever had to do was watch and feel my daughter going through so much pain and grief. But over the past seven years, I have seen enormous personal growth in Amy. She has grown so much in confidence; a warrior has emerged. The obstacles she has had thrown at her over the years have often caused her to sink. However, with her positive outlook, determination and humour, she has become someone to be reckoned with!

At the funeral, I was so proud of the way Amy was able to give such a beautiful, moving eulogy about Joe. She showed me how much strength of character she has and resilience beyond I thought possible after such a personal tragedy. I myself, have never felt such grief as I have from Joe's death. I am so incredibly proud of my daughter of getting to where she is today. Joe would certainly be so proud, too.

Love you always.

Christine Iskra
Mum

The sudden, unexpected loss of your soulmate is a trauma that nobody wants to imagine or face. I have watched with awe as Amy battled through such darkness with grit, determination and hope. She is the epitome of true courage. I am so proud of my sister for continuing to dream, plan and create the best life possible for her family. Amy's journey over the past seven years can be exemplified by 20th-Century author, Anais Nin's words: *"Life shrinks or expands in proportion to one's courage."*

Love Kate.

Kate Van der Beeke
Sister

Amy Williams showed the world what she was capable of at Joe's funeral.

We all held our breath while Amy told us their love story, about the man only she knew, their travels, their friends and the memories they shared, and of course - their children.

Amy told us it had occurred to her that she was now a *"single mother"*, and she had so many questions. Mainly, what was she going to *do*?

We watched Amy *do* so much.

I admire Amy so much for all the things she took on. The way she navigated through selling the business, Joe's insurance, finances, shares, home renovations and her own re-education.

All whilst providing for the needs of her three children, which hasn't been a direct path and indeed not easy; Amy has managed to do what is best for them. She is an excellent Mum.

Amy has become a confident, self-sufficient, organised Entrepreneur, and she isn't afraid of hard work.

Terri Smith
Stepmother

It is my belief that the people you meet in your life are either there for a mere passing moment or, to stay for a while to teach you something or transform you. Others stay with you, travelling side by side or from a distance as you journey through your life. Amy and I met at an early age and have always remained close, even though our lives have taken different paths along the way. When Amy met Joe, it only took a few years before they became inseparable. There was definitely a force stronger than themselves that brought them together, kept them together and separated them in such a cruel way.

Shock, disbelief, anger, devastation, sympathy and an overwhelming need to protect were the sequence of emotions I felt when I heard of Joe's passing. All I wanted to do was to talk to Amy, to be by her side, hold her and take her pain away. I was respectfully aware of the shock she must have been in and not wanting to overwhelm her, so after making contact, I waited. I paced. I tried to move forward in a daze. The magnitude of the life-changing event had not yet entered our reality.

I watched Amy just surviving while trying to keep it together for the benefit of her young children. I watched her family and friends picking up the pieces around her, so she could grieve, all the while heavily grieving themselves. She made the choice to be selfless, and as the months passed, I witnessed a true warrior rise from the devastation and became a poster girl for resilience!

Amy has a tattoo of a warrior, and I have a tattoo of an infinity symbol entwined with the word balance. It is my belief that everything happens in duality and darkness comes into your life to show you how much love and strength is within your soul. Amy has certainly been thrown many challenges over these past seven years, raising three children as a single mother, and I know she has gone to some dark places during these times. But once again, her inner strength and resilience bring her back to her light, her true purpose.

Lyndal Wade
Close Friend

Amy is one of the strongest and most patient women I have ever met. After everything she has been through, she would continue to make her family's home a safe and happy place for her children to be raised in.

The favourite part of my job was dinner time. I would get to cook, and they would sit around the table as a family. This brought me so much joy. I watched as Amy listened to all of the kids' stories about their days. She never rushed them or interrupted, and she was always present and encouraging. There was always lots of giggles.

Little did I know I would get so much more than a job when I started working for the Williams' family in 2015. I would gain a second family. I would create three very individual bonds with three of the most loving and caring kids.

I would also gain a strong friendship with a woman I have a lot of respect for. One who I admire and one who continues to make me want to be a better Mother and Wife.

Kobie Leahy
Nanny and Close Friend

I started dating one of Joe's best mates (Adam - who is now my fiancée) only three short months after he had passed. Although I never had the chance to meet Joe, I have been told by so many people what an amazing human he was, and in a way, all the beautiful stories I have been told, have made me feel like I did know him. I was instantly drawn to Amy's courage and strength, and although she mentions that she HAD to be strong because of her three beautiful babies, I truly believe she is a fighter and that she was always put here to shine her light - even when she was faced with a tragedy that could have completely dimmed her light forever. I may have not known Amy before she became a grieving widow, but this lady has inspired me on so many levels over the past seven years with her beautiful, positive and generous energy. She is wise beyond her years and a true beacon of light for all of us. It is a privilege to walk this path with you Amy.

Karin Wolski
Friend

I have known Amy for nearly thirteen years. Our eldest children were newborns and we embarked on the motherhood journey together, through sleepless nights and endless milestones.

The morning I received the text message about Joe's death was surreal. I called a mutual friend and we discussed it and convinced ourselves that sadly it must be true, there is no way this could be considered a joke.

Even today it still feels unbelievable that this could happen to my dear friend. Amy has shown the world how to show strength alongside vulnerability, growth with resilience. She has made a conscious decision to not be defeated or defined by this tragedy. Amy has used this opportunity to prove to herself that perseverance has allowed her to become who she is today, despite her struggles.

Coralie Pinney
Close Friend

I've known Amy and Joe since I was a teenager. As far back as I can remember, they were together. There is no memory I have with either of them that doesn't include the other. As sure as the sun rises each day and the waves lap the shore, they were supposed to be together.

Blonde, adventurous, fun and faithful. They were in so many ways the quintessential couple.

Joe's sudden passing had a profound effect on everyone. I was so unsure how Amy would survive such a tremendous and shocking loss. I have watched her navigate the last seven years with such grace, strength and insurmountable courage that inspires me in so many ways.

Amy is a truly phenomenal human being who shares her light and love with the world, and I'm honoured to call her my friend.

Karen Holmes
Friend

I have had the great joy and privilege of being the family GP and GP Obstetrician for Amy and her family since 2005.

Supporting her through these times of new life and loss of life, love, and tragedy has allowed me to see firsthand what a resilient, loving young woman she is.

Amy built a beautiful, young family with her teenage sweetheart, Joe, before losing him tragically. They held a unique, loving bond between each other that they shared with young Henry, Ruby and Mia. The depth of love between them all made the sudden unexpected loss of Joe so distressing for Amy. The disbelief and devastation were eased only by the outpouring of support and love from her extended family and friends.

To be able to cope so bravely when left alone with her young children and her broken heart; to get up each day and go on caring for the children and helping them deal with their loss while trying to manage her own; to survive and thrive, was a testament to her resilience, her willingness to seek and preparedness to accept help from those around her, and to her love for her children.

Her journey has been hard and bumpy; her spirit strong and courageous.

She is an incredible woman, for whom I have the greatest admiration and respect.

Dr. Maria Kailis
MBBS DRANZOG GAICD

In 2014, I met an incredible woman named Amy Williams. Through our daughters' friendships that were fostered by attending the same school, I immediately gravitated toward Amy due to her happy-go-lucky, genuine and sunny approach to life.

We became very good friends quickly, and Amy shared her story of grief and challenges that she faces due to the sudden loss of her late husband Joe and the daily obstacles that arise due to being a single mother of three children – two of which have special needs.

It amazes me that Amy has reared such beautiful children alone. I have felt nothing but inspired by her ability to always look on the bright side of life – always smiling and never complaining about the cards she has been dealt with by the universe.

Amy's friendship and support have become a mainstay in my life, and I always feel uplifted by her company because of her tenacious nature. I am so proud that Amy has shared her story and her strength in words that come from her heart.

She is unique, strong and beautiful. I believe that everywhere she speaks, millions could resonate with her message.

Your friend for life.

Kate Hansen
Friend

Dedication

To my husband, Joe Williams, for giving me the most incredible 20 years. For without you, I wouldn't be the woman I am today.

To my beautiful children, Henry, Ruby and Mia.
For without your beautiful souls, I wouldn't know the meaning of unconditional pure love, compassion, empathy, patience and understanding.

Also, in loving memory of:

Nigel Williams, "Grumps"
and
George Jackson, "Gramps"

2009

2017

xx

A Miracle Within

If you want to be seen, first you need to see yourself.
If you want to be heard, listen to yourself.
If you want to be loved, love yourself.
If you want to receive, give to yourself.
If you want to be accepted, accept yourself.
If you want happiness, seek happiness within yourself.
If you want freedom, free yourself.
If you want sunshine and lollipops, find your inner sweetness.
YOU were the pillar of hope when you were born.
YOU were that miracle that grew inside your mother's womb.
And YOU are still that miracle.

— Amy Williams

Contents

Introduction	1
Prologue	5
Chapter 1: I Always Knew I Would Marry Him	11
Chapter 2: Doing Life Together	23
Chapter 3: Buried Deep	51
Chapter 4: Standing Still	59
Chapter 5: Life Goes On	75
Chapter 6: Drowning	93
Chapter 7: Treading Water	103
Chapter 8: Through A Widow's Window	115
Chapter 9: Dreaming Underwater	127
Chapter 10: Rising Above	133
Chapter 11: Embracing Emotions	143
Chapter 12: Inspired To Swim	149
Conclusion	153
Afterward	155
Acknowledgments	159
The Grief Survival Guide	163

Introduction

A couple of years ago, I had an epiphany that I was going to write a book. I was meditating down at the beach, and the image of a book came into view, and these words appeared:

"I always knew I would marry him..."

My negative ego played a good part for a long time, however. It told me that I'm not anyone special, that death occurs to everyone, every day, and why would anyone want to read about my life?

I believe the universe sends us what we need at the time or pulls us away from things if it's not the right time. For me, a couple of years ago, I wasn't quite ready to write a book.

I still had more learning to do. I still had more letting go to do. I still had more healing to unfold.

We will all suffer grief and loss in our lives; it is inevitable and an undeniable fact. Yet, no one talks about grief. No one knows how to talk about grief. It is avoidance the whole way - until it happens to you, then...

Boom.

You're in the thick of it, and there is no manual to help you climb out of it.

And so, I had to shove off my negative ego and tell it where to go; because I do have a story to tell. I do have wisdom to share. I do want to be the voice of grief.

SINK or SWIM

I *do* want to help others going through grief.

My book is called *SINK or SWIM* because my journey over the past seven years has taught me so much about resilience, determination and strength. I want to offer support, encouragement and inspiration to anyone who has been through grief, trauma and loss. It is my version of a heart-warming, raw and an honest personal story of how I have navigated my way through life; either sinking or swimming.

Maybe you know someone close to you that is grieving, and you don't know what to do or how to help them?

Together with my personal journey, my book includes a *Grief Survival Guide*. It covers all the things I learned along the way and all the things I wish I had known at the time. It gives practical to-do advice, from creating routines and diary management to learning all about grief and the emotional layers. I offer techniques and strategies to cope with the rollercoaster of emotions.

We all face challenges in life. Mine's no different. But if I can inspire, if I can show people my way of moving forward in life after a tragedy; that means the world to me, knowing that I've helped inspire someone else.

I don't believe I'm special or different from anyone else that has grieved or has lost a loved one. But I do know that I have made my own choices to live my life as happy and as free as I possibly can. And I did make the choice to move forward, to be inspired, to have projects on the go that gave me future goals. I was able to achieve and thrive.

This is my story of grief, love, hope and dreams.

You've got this, and I've got you.

With Love,
Amy x

Prologue

Tuesday, 18th June 2013.

"Daddy, wake up! Open your eyes, Dad!" said Ruby.

"Why isn't Dad opening his eyes?" Ruby asked Henry.

"Muuuum!" yelled Henry, *"Dad's not waking up!"*

Henry and Ruby were stomping down the hallway towards my bedroom. I sighed and wondered why the hell he wasn't responding. He would usually play-tackle them and get them breakfast. I walked out to the lounge room area faster than usual.

Then I saw him.

He was lying on the lounge room floor. He was on his back. As I kneeled beside him, I knew something was wrong.

I screamed his name, *"Joe! Joe!"* slapping his face, shaking him, saying, *"No, no, no, no, no, no!"* screaming over and over again.

SINK or SWIM

The utter shock. Oh my god, he's not responding.

"Joe!" I screamed again. His eyes were closed, but he's not asleep. Oh god, what is happening?

I had to run back to my room to get my phone, the longest run down the hallway and back, in an absolute panic, knowing that time was of the essence.

I gathered myself and went into *practical mode*. Okay, I need to call an ambulance.

"Triple 000, how can we help you?" said the operator.

"It's my husband! He's not breathing!" my voice was shaking.

"My kids are here, please hurry!"

I was on autopilot, I gave them my address very slowly and calmly. I went through all the questions the operator asked me:

"Roll him on his side and check his airways."

I tried, but I couldn't move him. He was too heavy.

"I can't!" I yelled.

"Can you see or feel if anything is lodged in his airway?" the operator asked.

I tried to put my finger into his mouth, but his jaw was stuck tight. I couldn't fit my finger in past his teeth:

"No, I can't! I can't get my finger into his mouth!"

"Do you know how to do CPR?" the operator calmly asked.

Prologue

"Umm, yes, but how many breathes to chest compressions?"

I didn't hear the answer. I threw my phone down and started CPR.

I held his nose and breathed into his mouth. All I could hear was gurgling. The sounds were awful, I was feeling sick already. I thumped his chest, but he was so hard it didn't feel like I was doing anything. Back to the breaths. Oh god, that awful sound.

Blood started to trickle out of his nose. I picked up my phone.

"Are you still there... Hello?" I asked the operator.

"Yes ma'am, I am still here."

"Um, there's blood coming out of his nose?"

Silence.

"Hello?!"

"The ambulance will be there very shortly, Amy."

"I could tell you forever how much I miss you and love you, but I will never get to hear you say it to me. That makes me feel so empty, miserable and alone. I can imagine your hug, but I can never FEEL it, I can imagine your laugh and smile, but I can never SEE it. I can imagine your voice, but I can never HEAR it."
~ Diary Excerpt

CHAPTER 1

I Always Knew I Would Marry Him

"If you want to be seen, first you need to see yourself."

It was 1990. I was in Year Eight at Lake Joondalup Baptist College, situated in the Northern Suburbs of Perth, where I first laid eyes on the popular, cute, blonde, surfer boy.

Joe was full of charisma, charm and good looks. I was drawn to him immediately. He had an aura to him and an energy that I wanted to be around.

He had plenty of girlfriends throughout high school. However, by the end of Year Nine, he finally noticed me. It was the end of school breakup, and we were on an excursion at Mullaloo Beach. With a cheeky smile, he said to me, *"Hey, Amy, nice bikini."*

SINK or SWIM

I blushed. I was wearing a peach bikini.

We had a brief summer romance over the 6-week school holiday break. By the time Year Ten had started, other boys were interested in me. Well, one in particular, Adam; he was *a bad boy*. He took me out to the movies, bought me dinner, and even a bracelet with my name engraved on it. My Dad loathed him. He knew what kind of boy he was, and he wasn't going to have a bar of him!

My parents had decided to take the boat out for the day, but I told them I had too much homework to do so I couldn't go. Instead, I spent the day with Adam.

We went to my friend Lyndal's house for a spa. We didn't stop kissing the entire time before Lyndal told us we should leave! The day ended with us kissing at the bus stop. My nosy neighbour apparently saw us and later dobbed me into my parents.

I got in so much trouble.

My Dad took a little visit over to Adam's and told him in not so many nice words to *"leave Amy alone."*

I can only imagine what his exact words were.

The following few weeks, Adam didn't talk to me and ended up having eyes for another girl. So, that was the end of that. Of course, at the time I was absolutely devastated. It took me quite a few months to get over. It was more because of the way he treated me towards the end, I felt like a fool and that everyone was laughing at me behind my back.

The following year in June 1993, a group of us girls camped the night at a camping resort called Club Capricorn in Yanchep for Marsha's 16th birthday.

It was about an hour's drive north of Perth. We excitedly piled in the van, chatted and giggled the whole way up with Marsha's brother driving us up there.

I Always Knew I Would Marry Him

We left the setting up of the tent to Marsha's brother, while we headed down to the beach. By the time we got back, he had lit a fire for us. The campground was pretty quiet, but there were two older guys camping right near us.

A few hours later, a couple of boys from our school turned up, Joe and Damian. They must have gotten word that us girls were camping.

We were all sitting around the fire, when the two older guys camping next to us came over. Joe started to introduce us all. I was standing next to Joe, so when he said my name, he casually put his arm around me.

I was waiting for him to take his arm away, but he didn't. We stood like that for some time, sharing stories around the fire.

After a few hours of laughter and being silly, we were ready to go to bed to finally get warm. We didn't know where Joe and Damian were meant to be staying, but they ended up in our tent. Joe said to me, *"It's really cold, hey. Sleep on top of me, and I'll keep you warm."*

Again, with that cheeky smile.

Sneaky, but it worked.

We were all in the tent together, so nothing happened - we didn't even kiss! But he did keep me warm all night, which was very nice.

The next school day, I plucked up the courage to ask Joe out. It was the end of the day and we were down near the lockers. I was so nervous!

With a shy look in my eyes, I said to him, *"You know what I'm about to you ask you, don't you?"*

He replied, *"Yes."* with yet another cheeky smile and just grabbed me and pulled me in for a kiss!

To say I was excited was an understatement! That afternoon I had netball training; I don't think I had ever been so full of energy before.

SINK or SWIM

Joe was a mad, keen surfer. He started surfing at the age of twelve. A few months into starting, he had a horrible accident landing on the surfboards fin. Luckily, he was wearing a wetsuit at the time, because it went straight into the top of his thigh.

I took up surfing myself when I was fifteen; I thought I'd go out and give it a go. One day, I remember I was out there on my foamy with the other surf school kids, and I spotted Joe out there. I was so excited to see him, because he was the best surfer ever! I started yelling out to him, *"Joe! Hey Joe, hi, it's me! Hi!"*

I think I embarrassed the hell out of him.

He turned around, gave me this little wave, and paddled off. Later, he laughed about that day. He said he was so embarrassed, the other surfers around him just kept shouting out to him, *"Hey Joe! Hey! Hey Joe!"*

They wouldn't leave him alone. But he laughed it off. He was pretty proud of me going out and surfing. He asked, *"You were doing really well. You stood up. Why didn't you keep at it?"*

I wasn't very good at keeping up with things. I liked it, but I never loved it. I let my fears get in the way. The waves were too big. I'd get held under, and I was too scared. Nah, that wasn't for me, but, I was happy to be a surfer's girlfriend... *His* girlfriend.

I sat on the beach for hours and hours on end, taking photos and videos of Joe surfing, like the good little surfer girlfriend. I got pretty good at it. I always knew exactly where he was out in the line-up.

Wherever Joe went, I went, but Joe wanted it that way. He was always happy with me coming with him on road trips. His mates probably hated it, because I was always the only girl, but he loved me being there with him. We didn't leave each other's side. We'd often go down to Albany for a weekend; pack the car on a Friday night to leave at 3am in the morning. They were the best getaways; the sunrise, the coffee, the music, the nature, and it just being us together.

I Always Knew I Would Marry Him

At the age of twenty, we hit a road bump. I was feeling neglected. Joe was surfing all the time. We decided to go our separate ways. We were both really upset and down about it, but we knew we needed to break up. I told him in my bedroom whilst listening to Madonna. I remember I couldn't listen to those songs again. I couldn't believe I was saying goodbye to him.

I was a mess. I took my dog down to the beach and just sat in the dunes and cried and cried and cried.

It took me a long time to feel okay.

I knew I needed to get myself together and move on. I had saved up a bit of money, and I was looking into going on a Contiki tour around Europe.

This was going to be the first time I was going to be out in the big wide world on my own. I'd only ever known Joe; hadn't been with anyone else and didn't really know how to be with anyone else. But that wasn't what it was about.

I wanted to find my independence. I wanted to be courageous and go out there to explore the world for myself.

A few months had passed before Joe contacted me. He wanted to talk. We met up after work one day, and he said, *"I really miss you, Amy. I want to give us another chance. I know I didn't prioritise you, but this time will be different. I will give up surfing if I have to."*

Whoa! Did he just say that? I never expected, nor wanted him to give up surfing. I knew he couldn't live without the ocean.

I wasn't sure how I felt with what he said. I was torn. On the one hand, there was my knight in shining armour coming back to me… But, on the other hand, I was excited about venturing out on my own.

That was my crossroads in life, right there. I knew that the decision I made would change the complete course of my life.

SINK or SWIM

I chose Joe.

It was about six months later, and I was going through a very sad and hard time. My parents decided to separate. It was such a shock for my sister and me; my parents had never fought in front of us. My world, as I knew it, was changing forever.

It was so hard seeing both of my parents in separate houses, living separate lives. My sister, two years younger than me, was 18 at the time. It was a very difficult time in a teenager's life to come to terms with. A lot of our friends had parents that had separated, but it had happened when they were very young. When you're older, you know and understand a lot more.

I was lucky I had Joe. He was there for me and supported me through my down times.

It was a few weeks after my 21st birthday, Joe and I were at Quinns Dog Beach, north of Perth. It was a wet and windy day, but before we left I sat him down and I said, *"Joe, I've been thinking…"*

His face looked a bit scared, but I carried on and said, *"Let's pack up and go around Australia!"* His face turned from scared to utter shock and joy all rolled into one.

He said wide eyed, *"Are you serious?!"* with a big grin and smile on his face.

I said, *"Yep, let's do it. I want to get away, we've had a shitty year and we both want to travel, so let's go!"*

As soon as we got back to my Mum's house in Kingsley, he started drawing up plans on how we would deck out the Cruiser. He tried his best to have his surfboards neatly tucked away under the decking inside the car, but after my input, they had to go on the roof rack. He was not impressed! But he knew I was right. After all, where was my wardrobe meant to go?!

We spent the remainder of the year planning and saving up. We were so excited and couldn't wait for this adventure together.

I Always Knew I Would Marry Him

The early days together – 18 years old

SINK or SWIM

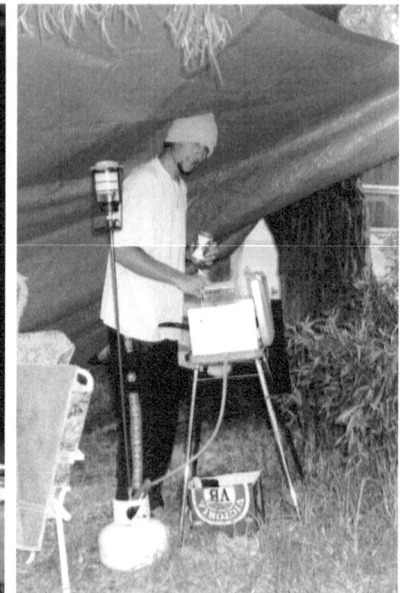

I Always Knew I Would Marry Him

Brad, Hannah, Amy, Joe – Hannah's birthday, 2007

"The family have been here every single night since you left. But soon, I will try a night on my own and see how I go. I'm scared of feeling lonely, and the realisation of you gone. I'm scared of forgetting. I deliberately try to remember all the small things, your smile, your wink, your hugs, your voice, your big beautiful manly hands. I'm so scared I'm going to forget."
~ Diary Excerpt

CHAPTER 2

Doing Life Together

"If you want to be heard, listen to yourself."

We spent three years travelling around Australia. We left Perth in April 1999 and came back in May 2002. We started our trip in our beaten-up, old, yellow Toyota Landcruiser, but we loved it! Our set up was very simple, but it worked. It did the job and got us to some incredibly remote places.

We hugged the coast pretty much the whole way around. Our days were spent in the sun; fishing, surfing, sunbathing, reading and exploring.

One place we loved, in particular, was Exmouth. We spent about four weeks in the National Park area and stayed at different coves for a few nights at each one.

SINK or SWIM

One of the coves, Osprey Bay, was where we spent two weeks. We were pretty much on our own for most of the time. Every day was magical, the warm sun, the crystal-clear water, the cool starry nights. Rather than sleep inside the Cruiser, we slept in the tent without the shade cover, so we could fall asleep looking at the stars - although we would get woken at the crack of dawn with the already warm sun belting down on us!

Being a National Park, there's heaps of exploring to do, especially around the river inlet of Yardie Creek. We drove down for a day trip because Osprey Bay was getting very windy.

There had been no surf for a couple of weeks, so Joe was getting a bit restless. He could see that there was surf pumping out at the surf spot at Yardies, which was two kilometres offshore from the river inlet. He was stuck though, because we had no boat to get out there, and there was no one else around to take him out.

However, that didn't stop Joe. What did he decide to do? He paddled out there, of course!

Yes, he was crazy, but also desperate to go for a surf. So, I had to sit on the beach, watch him paddle out to this surf spot, in shark-infested waters that I couldn't even see through binoculars.

He'd been gone for about half an hour, and I thought I'd go for a swim. I started walking into the water, but then literally right in front of me, I saw all this splashing. I thought, what the hell is going on there?

And then I saw the fins. Two sharks were having a feeding frenzy over a school of fish.

It completely freaked me out because there's Joe, two kilometres off the coast, surfing all on his own. There was no one else out there.

Two hours went by, and I was getting worried, but there was nothing I could do. So, I just sat there and had to wait. Finally, I could hear a motor in the near distance. I faintly saw a boat coming towards the shore, and

Doing Life Together

I thought, *"Oh, thank God. Joe's got a lift in."*

I was so relieved to see him. I asked him how it was. He gave me a nervous half-laugh, and he said, *"I saw a shark. It was heading straight towards me when I was duck diving through a wave."*

The guys in the boat happened to be trawling for fish not far from where Joe was surfing, so he waved at them to get their attention. Luckily, they saw him, and asked him, *"Where's your boat, mate?"*

He laughed. And replied, *"Oh, I don't have one. I paddled it."*

They were in stitches laughing, they could not believe he'd paddled two kilometres on his own to get a surf.

They said, *"Are you crazy?!"* and he replied, *"No, just desperate."*

We actually did spend some time inland. And that was exploring the Kimberley's untouched wilderness along the Gibb River Road. This unique 4WD track is 660 kilometres of corrugated red dirt. You must be fully prepared before venturing on this trip, with at least 2-4 spare tyres. We saw many caravans pulled over with blown tyres and no spare, or they had already used their spares. The road was graded only twice a year, which makes it an extremely bumpy ride for majority of the time.

The scenery was breathtaking, but the drive was horrendous! The non-stop shaking and rattling of the nuts and bolts and all the other car bits, including us, was very exhausting. We eventually got to the most beautiful place called Bells Rapids. We decided to stay there for the night, but little did we know, we had to book a spot in advance.

We pulled up at a nice little grassy area, started to unpack our Cruiser, and a lady comes over, and says, *"Excuse me, these spots are taken. You need a special permit."*

It was getting late and we were so tired from the drive. All we wanted to do was set up and go to bed!

She saw we were exhausted and said, *"Well, I'm looking for a bit of company. So, if you can camp down that way a bit, then you can stay in my area."* She was pointing to an area about forty metres away from her van.

Later that night, we sat around her fire and chatted for quite a few hours. She introduced herself as Iris. She definitely had some crazy stories to tell. Apparently, she was very good friends with INXS', Michael Hutchence. After weeks of being in her company, we begged to differ! We wondered why she was out in a remote area on her own, as she didn't seem very well equipped, nor from what we felt, wanting to be on her own.

The next day she asked if she could tag along with us, as she felt unsafe being by herself. We didn't mind at first, but after a few nights we'd had enough and just wanted to be on our own.

We couldn't wait to explore the Bungle Bungles. She mentioned that she couldn't get out there because her van wouldn't make it. So, we thought that would be a good time for us to part ways. But she had other plans.

Iris pleaded with us to take her. It was somewhere she really wanted to visit, and it would mean she would miss out on seeing them if we didn't take her. We gave each other the same roll of the eyes and really weren't overly keen to take her because she was starting to take advantage of us. But we saw no way out of it and not wanting to hurt her feelings, we reluctantly agreed.

Before we left, she parked her van at the entrance to the National Park road, and then commenced to pack nearly all of her belongings in bags to bring with her! We were so annoyed! We travelled as light as possible and there she was throwing in half her van of stuff.

The drive into the Bungle Bungles was a couple of hundred kilometres. It was breathtakingly beautiful. Iris had to lay down in the back of the Cruiser the whole way. It would have been extremely uncomfortable! We found a nice camp area and set off exploring. We slept in our Cruiser and Iris had her tent. We kept to ourselves that night and got a feeling she knew that we were a little bit annoyed she was with us.

Doing Life Together

It was a long, quiet drive back out the next day. We took her back to the van and said to her, *"Look, we're going to head off now. We've got a friend in Wyndham that we're going to go see."* We said our goodbyes and we couldn't wait to get going and finally just be on our own.

Then she said, *"I'm heading that way, too. So, I might see you on the way?"*

We gave her a half smile and literally jumped so fast into the car.

We gave each other that same look and I said to Joe, *"Go! Go! Go! Quick, we need to lose her!"*

She was beyond clingy. The wilderness is a place to get away and be with nature and enjoy the serenity… but we couldn't with Iris around! We were over it and it was so consuming that we just couldn't enjoy our time.

We quickly took off before she could even load her van back up. We didn't really go straight to Wyndham. We stopped at the top of a lookout as it was getting close to sunset. By the time it was dark, we high-fived each other and celebrated that she had probably driven straight past us.

The next day, we made our way to Wyndham. We stopped off at one of the little rock holes for a quick swim. We pulled up, and what do you know? We saw her van.

We literally screamed and laughed at the same time, turned around and went back out the other way!

We drove straight to Wyndham, parked at our friend's house, and finally, we had lost her.

Our most favourable and memorable time travelling around Australia was being in Darwin. We lived there for twenty months and met some amazing friends; friends for life.

Joe actually met them out in the surf - believe it or not. There happened to be a cyclone nearby that had whipped up some waves. Joe was out there, of course, and I was sitting on the cliff watching him. All of a sudden, three other guys with surfboards headed out there. I was really relieved to see there were some other blokes out there with him.

Afterwards, Joe came in all stoked and happy. He told me the guys had offered for us to go over their place for a barbeque that night.

We became best mates with Hoges, Simo and Chooka. We had some really fun times. From playing tennis, and swimming in the local pool, to making murder mystery videos, endless nights at the pub, and them surfing in crocodile-infested waters.

After surviving two wet seasons in Darwin, we needed to get out of there. If you stay in Darwin too long, you really go a bit crazy. However, our good, old, trusty yellow Cruiser would not get us much further, so whilst we were working and saving, we bought a newer Landcruiser to finish our Australia trip with.

That one got us all the way to Cape York and back to Perth, a year later.

When we were in Victoria, we stayed with Hoges, Simo, and Chooka for about a month. They showed us around their home town of Korumburra, down to Cape Paterson and all of its fabulous beaches.

That is where Joe proposed to me; on Powlett Beach.

It was Valentine's Day, 2002. The sun was setting, and we'd had a beautiful day down the beach. He was sitting behind me and just popped out a ring and said:

"So... You wanna get married?"

It was very Joe-style, totally low key! But I was so, so happy. I was even more delighted with that fact that he had chosen my ring. However,

Doing Life Together

as I was the receipt and budget controller, certain expenses can be accidently found out!

I absolutely LOVE surprises. I have done ever since my 16th birthday surprise party, which was a huge surprise to me! So, when I found a receipt in Joe's wallet for a large sum and the word *'ring'* next to it, I was devastated that I'd found it!

I remember being so angry at him for keeping that in his bloody wallet. But, I didn't want him to know that I knew, so for weeks and weeks I had to keep it to myself! When Valentine's Day was coming up, I already had an inkling that he would propose. I actually didn't tell Joe about the receipt for about another 10 years after.

South Australia was filled with beautiful, sunny days and star-filled nights. We lit campfires, we cooked yummy roasts in the camp oven, Chooka on his guitar; they really were some of the best times.

Luckily, Joe survived the shark-infested waters that he loved to surf in. It was May 2002; we finally made our way back into WA.

After we got married in March 2003, we only lived in Perth for a short amount of time. We made plans to do more travelling, starting with Southeast Asia for a few months of backpacking, and then onto the UK. We ended up living in Horley, near Gatwick Airport for nearly two years.

Whilst having our full-time day jobs, we started up our own surf travel booking agency called Surging Waters. We met up with a friend, Shayne, who was looking for an investor in an 80ft charter boat in the Mentawai Islands of Indonesia.

After a lengthy discussion about the risks involved (mainly sending money to an unknown boat builder in Indonesia), we did what we usually did in an unfamiliar situation... We flipped a coin!

It came up heads, which was the decision to go for it.

I remember we just looked at each other and said, *"Well, this is it. We're doing it!"*

We were so excited. In that instant, we decided that we were going to send all of our savings we had over to Indonesia, and not really know what we were getting into.

About six months later, we had an amazing, beautiful boat called Kaimana, ready for her first voyage.

After months of promoting and marketing our business in the UK, we managed to get a group of professional surfers on board from Cornwall. Being our maiden voyage, Joe and I naturally had to go out to make sure it all ran smoothly.

That was my first experience out at these magical islands. Ten days of complete luxury; all fully catered, including food, drinks, crew, and of course, the surf guide. The feeling of cruising crystal clear waters beneath us, whilst fishing, surfing, sunbathing, watching movies, sleeping, reading, and having all meals prepared and cooked for us... It was such an overwhelming feeling of amazement that *we did this* - we made this happen! It's our boat, it's our business, and here we are entertaining our first group, and seeing and witnessing them absolutely stoked about it, every single day.

It was pure joy and bliss right there for Joe and me.

We owned Kaimana and ran Surging Waters for ten years, even whilst travelling throughout Europe and Central America.

We did loads of travelling when we were living in the UK. We took off in our van around Europe for five months.

One of my favourite places we ever visited was Morocco. It was absolutely breathtaking. The culture, the colours, the weather; it really was an amazing place to be.

Doing Life Together

We snowboarded, Joe surfed, our days were spent exploring, relaxing, reading, and enjoying our freedom. Where else on earth can you surf in the morning then snowboard in the afternoon?!

Sure, the surf was early in the morning. The drive up the mountains was very long - with narrow roads that made me feel car sick with all the constant winding – but, we reached the top of the mountain late afternoon and headed straight for the snow with our snowboards.

I was a very beginner snowboarder... This was not a good idea. The snow was like ice. I skidded down on my butt nearly the whole way down, dodging rocks that were sticking out. I got to my feet towards the end, but fell onto a hidden rock, cutting my knees open.

Joe was still carving it down the mountain. When he eventually made it down, the operators told Joe they would put me on a donkey to take me back to our van because I couldn't walk. That way Joe could get in more snowboarding time. My face, when Joe got back to our van, said it all! He really tried hard to hide his laugh, but he couldn't help but crack up about my donkey ride.

The only awful thing that happened to us (luckily) was in Barcelona. We had a feeling we were parking in a dodgy area, but it was so hard to find our way around and park the van anywhere.

Two hours later, we came back from walking around, and the van had been broken into. It felt like such a violation, considering it was our home at the time.

They took my entire wardrobe, everything! Not Joe's crappy clothes, but mine. They took blankets, the pillows, and the duck down feather doona, and did I mention, my *whole bag* of clothes?! All I had were the clothes I was wearing; that was it.

Strangely enough, they left the snowboards, the electronics, and all the other tubs of stuff. They would have got more than they bargained for though, as they would've found my sex toy hidden in there!

I didn't bother replacing all of my clothes. I was angry for months, realising all the nice clothes I had lost. We did, however, have to buy a lot more warm bedding.

After our 5 months in Europe, as soon as we got back to the UK, we sold our beloved van, so we could then head off on our next trip, which was through Mexico and Central America!

Off we went on our next adventure! It really wasn't much of a holiday, though. It was a massively long trip all the way down to Panama, travelling from Baha California, Mexico, Guatemala, El Salvador, Honduras, Nicaragua and Costa Rica.

We tried our best to learn Spanish, although Joe relied mostly on me to do that part. Nicaragua will always hold some fond memories for me. That is where we conceived Henry! After a few days of feeling very sick, I bought an over-the-counter pregnancy test (attempting to ask in my best Spanish!).

The day I found out was the same day we were crossing into Costa Rica. The border crossings were long, stressful and usually expensive. I waited to tell Joe until the end of the day at a restaurant where we were having dinner.

Joe's face, initially was just complete shock and disbelief. I told him that the hotel room and the rum wasn't the best idea, after being van-bound and having friends travelling with us for the entire time. I guess it was inevitable!

Even after several weeks, Joe still had trouble believing it. He made me get about five different tests and go to the doctor and get an ultrasound that actually confirmed I was pregnant, then he let it sink in that we were having a baby.

The first person I told was my sister. Kate and Adam were in England at the time. She was so ecstatically happy for us. So, there I was, pregnant, travelling through third world countries in a smelly, hot motorhome that kept breaking down.

Doing Life Together

While our other friends went off and travelled down a beaten track to yet another amazing surf spot, we were stuck at a petrol station trying to get the van fixed. We slept in the van, in a petrol station, on the main road. It was awful, hot, and it stunk of petrol fumes; the men stared at me all day because all I could do was sit in a camping chair in the cool spot of the garage, and even then, it was 35 degrees in the shade.

I was so sick. I couldn't stand the smell of the food or the cooking. I got down to 52kg, and the doctor in Costa Rica told me to eat more. He demanded and pointed to Joe, *"You make sure she eats, she needs to eat."*

I just couldn't stomach anything.

We finally sold the van, which took months to do. The van needed a new carburettor that was not available in the whole of Central America. At one point, we thought we would just have to bail, and leave it on the side of a road somewhere and get out of there. But we desperately needed the money to get home.

We eventually found a buyer on *Craigslist* who lived in the US. His Panamanian girlfriend, who did not speak a word of English, met us in Panama City to do the swap over. That was an absolute mission, trying to find her and converse with her in our limited Spanish. We met her in a public place, and she gave us the cash in an envelope. Joe was on-edge with that much cash on him. Next minute we turn around, and she's gone! We honestly thought we had been set up to be robbed. We were shitting ourselves walking through Panama City back to the van.

The original plan was that she would come with us to the van and drive it to a town where her US boyfriend would meet her. It all sounded very strange, but we were so desperate to sell it.

Eventually, the US buyer got in touch with us and told us where to park it, as he had a friend who would take the keys from us.

Finally, we could leave Panama! It had been way too long; we were so exhausted from selling the van that we couldn't wait to get out of there.

SINK or SWIM

We packed up but had to leave a lot of stuff in the van. We got to the airport at 4am for our flight to Cuba, where we were meeting up with our friends once again.

Our bags were checked through, then immigration... There was a problem. We had overstayed our visa by *one* day! At the border from Costa Rica to Panama, the visa stated 60 days; however, that rule had since been changed to 30 days. We had been in Panama for 31 days. What a nightmare.

We had to pay a fine, and they told us we needed to go back into the city to the immigration office to get a new visa. It was only 5am, and the office wouldn't open until 9am. We had to wait for our luggage to come back off the plane, get another taxi into the city, and managed to get our hotel room back for a few hours of sleep.

I couldn't afford to lose my mind at this stage. I mustered up all my energy, strength and determination to face the officials at the immigration office. There were hundreds of people there. We took our ticket and waited for our number.

A few hours passed, and the numbers were all over the place. The knock-on effect this would have if we didn't make the next flight at 3pm would be huge.

I knew I had to get us on that next flight. I got up and walked past the crowds of people at the front line, knocked on the manager's door, and said in my very bad broken Spanish: *"Lo Siento, estoy embarazada, por favor, ampliacion de viados, vamos a volar hoy, tres tardes."* – translating to - *"I'm sorry. I'm pregnant. Please, we need our visa extended, we need to leave at 3pm today."* - meanwhile making ridiculous hand gestures of a plane flying in the sky.

She looked at me with no expression; no smile, no frown either, just blank. I thought we were screwed, and that she didn't understand. She mumbled something in Spanish.

Doing Life Together

All I heard was *"passport"*, so I handed them over, and with a big thud, stamp, stamp! That was it. She shooed us *"Goodbye!"* in English!

Thankfully, we made the 3pm flight to Cuba.

After travelling through third world countries for seven months, I was done. Arriving back into the US was like a breath of fresh air. The travelling still didn't stop there, though. We continued, but this time in a nice, everyday car and staying in motels.

We visited the Grand Canyon and Las Vegas, where we met up with Kate and Adam. They had just got engaged.

We drove to San Francisco, enjoyed the best seafood chowder ever (and I don't usually like seafood chowder!), and spent our last three weeks in Hawaii. Oh, so blissful. It was so lovely and relaxing.

By this stage, I was five months pregnant. We were staying in a backpackers and had our own room, which had the most amazing balcony that looked out over the ocean.

The Surfing Pipeline Masters was on; all the top surfers were there. It was a perfect atmosphere to be down on the beach and see Kelly Slater, amongst others.

We finally got home on New Year's Eve, 2007.

We settled back into Perth life, with our now three babies. Henry in May 2008, Ruby in December 2010 and Mia in November 2012.

When I was pregnant with Mia, we started on some significant renovations on our house in Wembley Downs. I would've been happy to leave it until the following year, but Joe was pretty adamant about getting it done. It was September, and Mia was due in November.

The work got started. It was a pretty crazy time living in a half-renovated home, with two kids, and a third pregnancy, but we made it work.

SINK or SWIM

Mia was born on 22nd November 2012. The house still wasn't ready. So, the kids and I moved in with my Dad and his partner, Terri. Luckily, they had a spare bedroom and took us in with two toddlers and a newborn for a month.

Joe spent most of his time at our house managing the renovation. Finally, the day before Christmas Eve, the house was ready to move in to.

Joe's pride and joy was the pool area. He had dreamed it, envisioned it, designed it and managed it from start to finish. I will never forget the day the pool was filled up.

It was March 2013, Henry, Ruby and I were the first ones to christen it. The look on Joe's face was complete admiration and satisfaction. He was so proud.

We had been planning this renovation and pool area since we bought the house three years earlier. So, for him, it was a dream come true. We were ecstatic to be enjoying this moment together as a family.

Although, as much as we loved our family life and being in our nicely renovated home, there were always future plans being made.

Travel. More of it.

Back when we were travelling around Australia, we talked about how we would love to take our (future) kids around Australia before travelling with them overseas. It was such a great experience for us, we could only imagine how amazing it would be offering that opportunity to our kids.

We had already gotten the ball rolling and were looking into a new setup. Would we choose a camper trailer or a pop-out caravan? So many choices to be excited about!

Bells Rapids, Gibb River Road, Western Australia - 1999

Fun in Darwin, Northern Territory - 2000

Engaged! Powlett Beach, Victoria – 2002

Afternoon sunsets, South Australia – 2002

Doing Life Together

The surfboard quiver of Joe, Hoges, Chooka
& Caesar, South Australia – 2002

Camp setup at Cactus, Penong, South Australia – 2002

Travel in convoy – 2002

Our boat, Kaimana, in the Mentawai Islands, Indonesia - 2005

Our green van that we travelled through Europe in – 2007

Soccer World Cup with Adam and Kate, Germany – 2006

The Donkey ride after my snowboarding fall, Morocco – 2007

Sunset on top of our Chevy van, Nicaragua – 2007

Doing Life Together

Our Chevy van always breaking down, Costa Rica – 2007

A few too many drinks after climbing Volcan Tajumulco, Guatemala – 2007

Flor de Cana Rum with our travel mate Adam, Nicaragua – 2007

Doing Life Together

Joe & Henry – 2010

SINK or SWIM

Joe & Henry – 2011

Joe & Ruby – 2011

Joe & Mia – 2013

Joe, Henry, Ruby & Amy in Busselton, celebrating our 10 year wedding anniversary – 2013

"The kids miss you SO much. Mia hasn't slept through the night since you passed. Your little Ruby Rubes, my god, my heart breaks for her. She was your little princess, you meant so much to her. She hasn't said much, but she knows, in her own way. The first few days she was asking, 'Where's Dadda? When's Daddy coming home? I want my daddy.'- but then she stopped. That broke me."
~ Diary Excerpt

CHAPTER 3

Buried Deep

"If you want to be loved, love yourself."

I didn't give up.

I knew if it was the other way around, Joe wouldn't stop. I opened the door for the paramedics. She said:

"Where is your husband?"

She followed me to the lounge room. I sat on the couch opposite him as she immediately started chest compressions. After a few, she stopped and calmly asked me to take the kids and myself outside. I asked her:

"Why?! Why are you stopping?"

She didn't answer me.

The other paramedic came rushing in. Again, she asked me calmly to step outside.

My next-door neighbour, Jarrad, was already at the front door and I just screamed in horror. I screamed:

"He's gone. He's gone..." over and over and over again.

He kept saying:

"Who? Who's gone?"

Alana, Jarrad's wife, took Henry and Ruby next door to their house. Mia was still in her cot sleeping. I was shaking in absolute shock, but also thinking:

"They will fix him. It will be okay. This cannot be happening. This is not how it's meant to be, not to us. Mia's only six months old. It can't be. It just can't. He can't leave me. He can't leave me, not with three kids, not on my own."

My brother-in-law, Adam, was then at my front door. Jarrad was talking to him. The feeling of deafening silence ringing in my ears, but with all this hustle and bustle of talking and noise.

I felt like I was going to faint but trying to keep it together. I just kept thinking, *"No, this is a dream. It's a dream. It's all going to be okay, it will all go back to normal."*

It was only 7.30am.

But that deep sick feeling in my stomach, bile rising up my throat, my stomach gurgling so loud - like it was grumbling out of hunger - but this was not hunger. This was adrenaline overload. This was deep utter shock. Something my body had never encountered before.

Buried Deep

Several police cars were on my driveway. Everything that went on in the house afterwards is unknown to me. But over the years, more information has emerged.

The police had to make sure there was nothing suspicious; just doing their jobs. We were all next door. The kids were fine, eating breakfast. Alana was looking after Mia.

I was sitting on the stairs inside Jarrad and Alana's house. I needed to phone my Mum.

"Hi Mum, it's me..." I said, trying not to be sick at the same time.

Mum replied:

"Oh hi, Amy! I was just about to leave to take Eric's Mum -"

I stopped her and said:

"Mum, I need you to come over... It's Joe... He's dead."

There was silence for a few seconds before Mum replied:

"Dead? What do you mean? What? Oh god, shit, Amy! Okay, I'm coming! I'm coming now!"

I don't even really remember my Mum arriving, nor my sister. Maybe half an hour had gone by, and my Mum and sister were sitting with me on the stairs. We were all in complete shock. My body couldn't cope. I had several trips to the toilet vomiting, then dry retching as I had nothing left in me.

Then I had the dreaded phone call to make. To Nigel and Julie, Joe's parents.

I had no idea what words were going to fall out of my mouth. I had no idea how I was going to say what happened. Nigel answered the phone.

"Nigel, its Amy." I said in a very low tone.

"Hi love!" he responded chirpily.

I froze. I didn't know how to continue.

"Nigel..." - big breath - *"Nigel, its Joe."*

There was silence.

Nigel knew, or at least he knew something was terribly wrong.

"No... No... No!" he yelled. I could hear Julie scream in the background. I could not get the words out. I couldn't bring myself to say the word *"dead".*

"Nigel, you need to come over. Just come over."

Two police officers came over to see me. They sat me down and said:

"Joe Williams, your husband, is deceased. We are very sorry for your loss."

The tall, dark-haired, blue-eyed police officer started talking about funeral homes and other things which I cannot recall. He said to me:

"Before he is taken away, would you like to see him?"

I immediately shook my head, "No, no, no. I can't."

The thought of seeing his stiff, lifeless body again was sickening.

But at the same time, when they said, *"Before he is taken away..."* I was screaming inside:

"No! Don't take him away...That means he really is gone... Literally, gone..."

It was so conflicting and heartbreaking, all at the same time.

Buried Deep

After a few hours of being next door, I went back home. By this time, all the emergency vehicles had left. I found out months later that it was the police first on the scene, not the paramedics. The female police officer was the one who did the chest compressions in front of me.

The tragedy had bought all the family together. My family and Joe's family. We were all just sitting around the dining table, not knowing what to say. Trying to comprehend what had just happened.

I was so numb. I couldn't cry. I was in shock, as with all of us.

The ripple effect of Joe's death was immense. Only hours had passed, and the word was spreading. The effect it had on everyone's life that day will never be forgotten. Every single friend, family member, colleague, and acquaintance all have their own story as to how it changed their lives forever. That one single moment of receiving a phone call or a message.

Some of Joe's mates were trying to get home from being away on holidays or working hundreds of kilometres away on the mines.

It was a huge shock for everyone that knew Joe.

Never ever in my life had I seen my Dad cry. Never had I seen my Dad emotional. Until the day Joe died.

After coming back from next door, I was in Mia's room, breastfeeding her and putting her back to sleep. As I stepped out of her room, I met my Dad in the hallway. His face white, eyes swollen, his body hunched over, *"What... What..."* shaking his head, trying to say, *"What happened?"*

"He's gone..." was all I could say. I just fell into his arms, and we both sobbed.

My Dad had been in an early meeting and was just about to go into another one at 9am. He checked his phone and saw several missed calls from 7.30am. My sister had left a message:

"Dad, its Kate. You need to come to Amy's straight away... Joe has died. Please drive carefully."

He drove straight past the office to my house all in a complete daze. The police met him at the door and guided him in towards the hallway and bedrooms, not the lounge area.

As a father, all he wanted to do was *fix it*. But he couldn't. He had to be strong for me but was also consumed with immense grief.

One phone call I did receive that day was from *Donate Life*. Hours after Joe's passing, and I had to answer a lengthy questionnaire all about him. It was so hard and uncomfortable to be talking about him that way. Still, Joe was adamant about being a donor. They were very supportive and told me I could stop at any point if it was getting too much. They needed to act quickly, so it was imperative the process was finalised.

We still didn't know how Joe had died. That was the worst part. We sat around the table, not knowing how he died, why he died, or what the hell had happened.

"Henry is making me so proud of him. Two weeks after you died, he started using his own legs to swing on the swing! You would've been so proud. You were always trying to get him to do it himself. I think he did it for you. I told him how proud you would have been."
~ Diary Excerpt

CHAPTER 4

Standing Still

"If you want to receive, give to yourself."

The following week up to the funeral, was such a blur, yet so busy. Unbelievable; the things that needed to be done. There was no time to sit around and mourn. From writing a eulogy, deciding on funeral songs, putting together photos for a slide show, the endless amounts of documentation needed to be signed and approved... All whilst breastfeeding a baby and looking after Henry and Ruby.

I was certainly not on my own, though. My whole family was there from day one and did not leave my side. I breastfed, and they would put Mia back to bed. I would be sitting on the couch, and lunch would appear in front of me. I had endless cups of tea, half drank mostly, but they kept coming.

I felt myself getting angry on the inside that it was just so bloody unfair. Why was he taken away so soon? So young, fit, healthy and the most amazing Dad and person ever.

Why Joe?

He had so much to live for, with three young kids. He needed to be there for them, and for me. We had plans and dreams, so much still to do as our completed family and house had just finished. We needed to be there together to enjoy it.

How could I possibly cope without him? He had been my whole life. Twenty whole years together. We'd just celebrated our tenth wedding anniversary.

How can he just vanish from my life just like that?

No warnings, no signs, nothing.

I had no chance to save him. I wish there could have been a sign or something. It's so, so bloody unfair. I know he would have fought like anything. If he had known he was dying, he would have done everything to stay alive. He would never have chosen to leave his beautiful children behind.

And to think, on that morning, I hadn't the faintest clue. I got up at 6am, fed Mia and went back to sleep. Meanwhile, he was lying out there dead already.

No warnings, no signs, nothing.

He always said he wanted it to be quick. That was all he wished for; a quick death. I would tell him to stop talking about it, but we both knew the risks of him surfing. So, maybe we were both aware that if he was to die, it would most probably be from a shark attack. I know he was a little bit worried about surfing on his own, especially late in the evening, or very early mornings.

Standing Still

We talked about how we would want to die together. We would just hate to be stuck in a hospital or be non-functioning. We both made a pact that we would not let each other be like that; in the end.

We talked about how we would take ourselves down to a beach. We would tie ourselves together with rope and have weights on us. We would walk out until the water was over our heads and hold each other until we both peacefully died together. As much as it sounds awful, that was how much we envisioned dying together.

A few nights before the funeral, my doctor, Maria, came to my house to talk to us about Joe's death. The cause of death was still undetermined, as it was pending further investigation of a post-mortem. However, she could say that it was heart related. That it was heart failure. That was all we knew at the time.

It was a long wait; two months before we found the actual cause of death. Focal Coronary Atherosclerosis was the final diagnosis, which is the hardening and narrowing of the blood vessels on the surface of the heart. It was suggested that possibly a piece of the plaque came loose and lodged in the artery, which caused the blood to stop flowing to the heart.

The very next day after Joe died, I was angry. I needed some space. I needed to be on my own. So, I went down to Scarborough beach. It was cold and windy, but the sun was out.

I walked up the beach a bit, made sure no one was around. I was so angry he left me. I stood on that beach, and I screamed and shouted into the wind:

"Why did you leave me? Why did you leave me!"

I screamed through my streaming tears over and over until I had exhausted myself.

Kate was walking up towards me. She was worried. They were all worried.

My beautiful family.

We just sat on the beach for a while and cried together.

She just wanted to make sure I was okay, I guess, and wasn't about to go and do anything silly. So many emotions, which were so confusing. I was so sad and so lost, but also just angry that he'd left me. And he'd left me with three kids on my own.

I couldn't believe he'd left me to do this all by myself.

I would get asked, *"Were there any warning signs? Was he sick? Was he complaining of anything?"*

I'd simply respond with, *"No, he was absolutely normal."*

I think back to the weeks before and wonder, *"Was there a sign? Was there something that I could have done?"*

But no.

Even my doctor said it would have been extremely quick.

Even if he'd gone to the doctor's the day before and said he wasn't feeling well, there's no way they would have referred such a young, fit guy to have a heart monitor test. There's just nothing that could have been done. The death itself was quick. I was told this by the medical practitioners and later down the track, by a psychic medium.

Strangely, Joe used to talk about that he wouldn't die old and that he didn't see himself growing old. He always told me he would die before me. And maybe it was because he mentioned it a few times that I believed it. But one thing I felt sure of, was that I strongly believed I would always know.

Standing Still

We had that soulmate connection where I would finish his sentences, or I'd say something he was just thinking about. He used to always comment on how much we knew each other and how in sync we were. I always felt like I would know if anything was wrong.

It was the day before the funeral. I decided to get a pedicure. I don't know why; it was June. I wasn't even going to show my feet. I was sitting in one of the massage chairs. Maybe it was the massaging moving my body, but as she was filing my toes, tears just started streaming down my face.

She thought that she'd hurt me. She was looking up at me, *"Oh, I'm so sorry. Are you okay?"*

I sobbed and sobbed, and through tears I said, *"It's my husband's funeral tomorrow."*

She just stared; pale faced. She didn't know what to say.

A lady was sitting next to me, getting her feet done. And she said, *"Oh, my gosh. I am so sorry to hear that."*

And I told her the story of what happened.

I needed people to know that here I am getting my feet done, but I'm saying goodbye to my husband tomorrow. It just doesn't make sense. It made me realise then and there, we could be walking past anyone and you just don't know what's happened to that person in their life; yesterday, today, or tomorrow.

The funeral was large. Hundreds of people packed Pinnaroo Memorial Service.

There are no words to describe what it was like driving from home to the cemetery in a limo; arriving and seeing hundreds of people spilling out of the chapel. I saw people that I hadn't seen in a long time, to then seeing the best of our friends.

The look on their faces; it was so unbelievable we were doing this. The pall bearers were six of his really good mates, Adam, Brad, Mike, Cam, Jarrad and Chooka. Their faces showed it all, pure heartbreak, utter devastation and complete shock.

As we walked in and sat down, I took a deep breath, and I thought:

"This is it. This is for everyone to say their goodbye."

The kids were there, but they were being looked after by family friends in a room offset from the main one. I wanted to concentrate on the funeral for Joe and for my friends. Two of his good mates, Adam and Jakub, said a beautiful speech, choked through the tears, along with everyone else.

Then it was my turn.

I heard the gasps of a lot of people when they realised I was getting up to talk. I understand most people would not be able to do that for their spouse. It would be just too heartbreaking. And obviously, it was, but already, I had felt a need in me to honour Joe and speak from my heart.

Everyone that knew Joe and I, knew how much love we had for each other. Our world was so full of adventure and life. I needed to share that. I had so many amazing things to say about my beautiful husband.

I found my inner strength and got through my eulogy. I heard many tears. Although, I didn't once look into the crowd, as I thought it might just crumble me:

"Joe, my beautiful husband.

You have been my rock for twenty years. No matter where we were and what we were doing, I felt so safe, happy and alive with you.

Standing Still

Your love for life, your energy, your motivation, your smile captured us all.

You had this unique ability to draw people into your infectious happy mood. Whether it was because you just had a good surf (or were allowed to go for a surf) or getting home and having Henry and Ruby run up to you yelling 'Daddy! Daddy!' full of smiles and laughter, and a beautiful grin from your baby girl, Mia. Or when we had mates around for a barbeque, you loved cooking your 'Joe-style' lamb cutlets - they also will never be forgotten.

Joe was so kind, generous and thoughtful. He was one of a kind. He was quite particular about a few things, like his beach towel, his wax tub and he didn't like sand in the car, house or near his surfboard, which is strange considering he spent half his life on the sand down the beach.

He was a perfectionist, which can be seen in the house. He would've driven Russell crazy, but that was Joe – it had to be perfect.

He had a vision. He was a good photographer, he knew which angles to capture, always capturing the mood.

He was a dreamer but also a do-er. If he had a dream, he was going to make it a reality.

He was an adventurer. Always wanting to push the limits to get somewhere further, deeper or where no-one else had been before.

You name it, Joe tried it. And annoyingly, was most probably very good at it. He was a warm and inviting person to be around.

From our younger days of me sitting on the beach watching you surf for hours and hours, to travelling the world with you, renovating houses, owning a boat in the Mentawai Islands, having three babies and creating two businesses, I would not take away one second of it.

SINK or SWIM

We knew each other so well that many times I would say something, and you would look at me with a smile and say, 'I was just thinking about that.' You always thought I had good intuition, but I just think it was our hearts and souls that were linked together as one.

Your beautiful heart gave way. Why you were taken from us so soon, we will never understand.

Maybe that's why you felt the need to pack so much into one lifetime, to live life to the fullest to explore to dream to discover. It's uncanny how the quote from Mark Twain was put on your surfing photo for the Australian Surf Life magazine.

My heart breaks, knowing you would never have wanted to leave us. That you weren't finished with your plans and ideas, living as our newly completed family of five. Even going through major renovations and a newborn, we were already talking about the next big trip – packing up the kids, buying a caravan and heading around Australia, again.

My heart will remain forever broken. I still feel you are with me and just hope our strong bond and connection will help me get through this and eventually, all I will remember, will be the good times.

I don't want to say goodbye, but I know I must. I will tell Henry, Ruby and Mia just how much you loved them and adored them; more than life itself. Your spirit is alive in them, I can feel that. As they grow, I will never let them forget the man you were, the man with dreams, love, respect and honour, a true gentleman.

You gave me so much love, happiness, memories, adventure and joy; and for that, I thank you.

Thank you for giving me YOU."

The next few hours after the funeral ceremony, were a blur. The wake was back at my house, and I remember one particular moment.

Standing Still

One of Joe's close friends from high school, a good mate of his, Marty, was standing on his own in tears. He looked devastated. I went up to him and gave him a big hug. I said, *"It's going to be okay."*

And he said, *"I don't know how you're doing it. I don't know how you're doing it, Amy."* And I just said, *"It's going to be okay."*

It wasn't all doom and gloom at the wake. I knew Joe would not want us sitting around, crying and pining for him. He was always the life of the party. He was always so happy and sociable. You could hear his voice miles away. Even pick it out in a crowd.

I loved the sound of his voice.

The house had never had so many people in it since the renovations. Joe would have been stoked. It was such a shame he missed it. The sun was shining, drinks were plentiful, music was cranking, tears were shed, stories were told.

For a moment, it felt like a great party. But the main person was missing. It was like being at a birthday party – without the birthday boy. It felt strange. I felt the deep hole of him missing.

A few days after the funeral, Cam, one of his good mates, organised a paddle out, down at Brighton Beach. It was the perfect day.

The sun was shining, and it was warm. The waves were pumping. Joe was definitely around. All his friends paddled out and joined a circle. We all threw flowers into the ocean to remember and celebrate him. Joe's surfboard accompanied the paddle out, his board was pushed into a big set.

After the waves had crashed and the board made it back up on the shore, it had broken in half. It seemed so fitting for Joe's board to break on that day.

SINK or SWIM

One of the hardest days was picking up Joe's ashes. Kate had offered to come with me, but it was something I wanted to do on my own. I needed to be with my own thoughts and emotions.

I drove to Pinnaroo and waited in the waiting room for a few minutes before being greeted. The feeling of being back there flooded my mind with such sorrow and emptiness. Joe had been by my side for everything in my life. Now, I had to stand strong on my own without him.

As they passed me the huge blue plastic container, I was taken aback as to how heavy it was. So much so, I nearly dropped it. I wasn't expecting that. But really, what was I expecting having never held ashes before?

On the drive home, I had him on the passenger seat. I was sobbing and felt sick.

I imagined him sitting there, next to me on the seat. I even reached my arm over and put my hand on the seat, feeling it, like it was on his leg. I kept saying, *"I'm sorry, bub. I'm sorry I couldn't save you."*

I pulled over into Trigg car park, just to sit for a bit. It was so exhausting, all this crying. It felt like this feeling would never end.

I walked in through my front door. Mum and Kate were in the kitchen. The look on their faces as I walked in with the plastic container also showed such sorrow and emptiness.

My way of dealing with it was not talking about it. I knew they wanted to comfort me, hug me and support me, and in turn, it would help them. But it was just too hard. I was exhausted from already being so distraught on my way home; that was enough emotional turmoil for the day.

His personal belongings were one of the hardest things to look at. His wallet. His wallet is just sitting there on my bedside table. How could he

Standing Still

be gone without his wallet? You don't go anywhere without your wallet. It just felt so unfathomable, staring at his wallet. What do I do with it?

For months, I couldn't take Joe's shoes away from the front door. To me, it truly meant he wasn't living here anymore. I didn't want to take him away from the house. I didn't want the kids to suddenly see parts of Joe no longer here. Despite that, his car had to be taken away. I couldn't bear to look at it.

I was constantly on a search trying to find everything and anything that was sentimental and meaningful about Joe. I would search through our photos, the video footage on the computer. And then… BOOM. His voice.

Hearing Joe's voice cut me so deep, I still have no words to describe it.

I was asked a few times, *"Do you ever feel like you expect Joe to walk through the door at any minute?"*

Strangely enough, it was always a *"No."*

I think after seeing him *very* dead, it was fixed in my mind that he was dead, and he wasn't ever coming home. I never had that feeling of expecting him any minute.

But what I did feel were situational triggers.

It would be as simple as the time. Around 5pm. This would have been the time Joe got home from work, and the kids would run out to meet him; we would share our days with each other.

Or when the gate would open, and I would hear the latch shut. I immediately thought of Joe walking through the gate.

Or when Ruby and Henry would run around naked after a bath, and remember Joe wasn't there to chase them, to laugh and giggle and say, *"I'm going to get you!"*

Or when Mum accidentally set another placemat at the table and quickly took the plate away, so I wouldn't see.

The house felt so empty without him. His energy was gone, and I felt it so intensely. His non-presence was the constant reminder that he wasn't here.

But, my amazing Mum always was. She was so strong for me. She just took over. She was organising a schedule of who would be looking after me, and who was going to sleep over. She was literally the captain of the ship. She just made everything happen. Everyone would contact mum to see what I needed.

Dad and his partner, Terri, were never far away either. It was so comforting to know my family were so close by. They would often pop over; Terri looking after the kids, Dad and I talking or just sitting there, not really knowing what else to be talking about.

Joe was like a son to my Dad. Every Saturday morning, for years, Dad and Terri would come over with the paper - two copies because Dad liked his own full paper not to be tampered with - and coffees. Joe and Dad would often talk about real estate, cars, boats or whatever current affairs were happening. I would be flicking through looking at the nice houses, and the pretty pictures, reading the horoscopes, not really reading the paper, just listening to their conversations. It always gave me a break to relax and have a coffee.

Terri would always be with the kids. She was amazing with them. She would play hide and seek, and puzzles, hot and cold, she loved it - and the kids loved it, too! We all looked forward to seeing Dad and Terri on Saturday mornings. It was one of our most favourite and cherished rituals.

Joe loved it so much because he knew, if he *needed* to go for a surf - or had already left early that morning - that I would have company, so I wouldn't be sitting at home by myself with the kids on a Saturday.

Cunning plan, Joe.

Paddle Out at Brighton Beach – June 2013

Amy & Hannah with Joe's broken surfboard

Joe's plaque resting on the rocks at Trigg Beach

Mural painted by Drew Straker on the outside wall of our home. Photo taken by Amy of Joe surfing in Morocco

"Every day, Henry asks about you, 'Why did Dad have to die? I miss Dad so much.' and would burst into tears. 'I wish dad was here.' Night time is the worst time for him. He cries every night and wishes you were here. My heart just breaks, and I cry with him. All I can say is, 'I know Henry, I wish he was here too.' Fuck, this is hard."
~ Diary Excerpt

CHAPTER 5

Life Goes On

"If you want to be accepted, accept yourself."

One thing I realised very quickly; life goes on.

Hours roll into days; days roll into weeks; all of a sudden, months have gone by.

I felt like everyone was moving on, but I was still stuck way back at day one. It was like I could see myself move throughout my day, doing, chatting, laughing, organising and looking like a normal person; but I felt so completely opposite of this on the inside.

It was like I was watching the shell of me move around, but inside I was standing still.

SINK or SWIM

I remember one moment I was in *Target*, shopping for new clothes for the kids. It had only been about three weeks. I was piling up the trolley, a lot of new clothes, for all three of them. As I was getting clothes off the rack, I stood there and thought, *"What the hell am I doing? What am I buying clothes for? My husband is dead, and I'm shopping for clothes."*

I looked around, saw all the people in their own world shopping for their clothes, and thought, *"They have no idea that the woman they're standing next to has just lost her husband."*

I walked over to the cashier, and she looked at my loaded trolley and cheerfully said, *"Getting a whole new winter wardrobe, hey?"*

I looked at her, and I said, *"Well, I've got three kids, and my husband just died."*

She didn't know where to look or what to say. And so, I said, *"He only died three weeks ago, and they need clothes."*

She just said, *"I'm really sorry."*

And that was that.

My husband just died, but here I am walking around the shops, doing normal things.

It just feels wrong. This feels wrong inside.

I remember the day I had to go to my private health insurance office with the ambulance bill, which was $900. I filled out some paperwork and showed her the bill.

As she was going through my questions, she said, *"Oh, you haven't put here... Which hospital did the ambulance go to?"*

I looked and stared blankly and blurted out, *"He went to the morgue."*

Life Goes On

The look on her face was one of shock, and sorrow all rolled into one.

I felt my heart beating faster. I felt bile rising up my throat. That was the first time that I'd said, *"The morgue."*

For some reason, it just made it all so real.

I was told to never make a big decision after you lose someone; to always wait at least a year. But I knew very early on what I needed to do with our business, Surging Waters. The boat, the surf, the lifestyle; it was Joe's passion - not mine. But, in keeping with the advice, luckily, we had a friend, who was also a business partner, take over from me for about six months, before needing to make the final decision of selling.

For ten years, I did the day-to-day running of the business, whilst bringing up the kids at home. It was a sad day for me to say goodbye when the right time came to sell. It was like my little baby that I'd had for a whole decade, and now it was time for me to walk away from it.

Saying that, after I'd made the decision, I felt a huge wave of relief. It was just another thing that I had to let go of after losing Joe.

I was however extremely lucky that two years prior, Joe had organised for us to have life insurance. We had the top cover because we knew we were going to extend our mortgage to renovate.

Earlier in the year, we discussed our insurance premiums. They were costing us too much. We called our advisor, but he said we had already paid them for that year, and we could look into reducing the level of cover from the following year.

Little did we know just two months later, I'd need that pay-out.

Unfortunately, we didn't have a Will, which caused quite a few issues and long delays.

SINK or SWIM

The insurance company wouldn't pay out until they had done their due diligence of making sure Joe had no previous ailments or issues with his heart.

It took just over two months to receive the final coroner's report.

I had mortgage payments to pay with no income. I would spend my days sending letters to the bank requesting that they stop payment. Everyone seemed to need the *Letters of Administration* because we didn't have a Will. The red tape is just huge.

It took months of writing letters, making phone calls back and forth to the coroner's office, the bank, the insurance company; it was so draining, and everything was done in very slow motion.

My family all put their lives on hold for me. Their own plans were forgotten and not even thought about. That is what family do, but they all made a sacrifice to ensure me and my kids were safe, happy and looked after.

At the time of Joe's passing, Henry was in pre-primary. After the funeral, it was decided that it would be best for Henry to go back to his normal school routine. I couldn't face the school, to begin with. The first day back, Mum, Kate and Julie (my mother-in-law), took Henry and dropped him at the school gate. That was one of the hardest days for Henry, he was in tears every single day.

Julie was very supportive and so good with the kids, especially helping me get Henry off to school. She was always just a phone call away to help out. I cannot imagine what my mother and father-in-law were also going through. Losing a child would be next-level grief. I didn't know what to do for them. I wasn't much help for anyone else.

My trips to the school were extremely hard, which brought around bouts of anxiety. My head would spin, I felt dizzy and sick and would find it hard to talk. I just wanted to get out of there. I felt like everyone was staring at me.

Life Goes On

I knew everyone knew and that they didn't know what to say to me. I knew everyone was looking at me and feeling so sorry for me. I felt like I was that accident that people stare at, not wanting to look, but can't help it. But I also knew everyone meant well.

It's a very surreal and strange experience when you are the *grieving widow*. You are that person that no one ever wants to be. You are that person that something so unbelievably tragic has happened to.

I couldn't believe that I was that person.

After a few short weeks, my good friend and builder, Russell, popped over. He knocked on the door and asked me how I was, and before I could answer, tears welled up.

I literally collapsed into his arms and could not stop crying. We both stood there for quite some time, shedding tears. I would like to say I hadn't cried so hard, but sadly, it was a very regular occurrence.

Sometimes, I cried so hysterically that it was near impossible to breathe.

I was crying because I didn't *want* to be doing it. I didn't *want* to be on my own. I didn't *want* a dead husband. I didn't *want* to bring kids up on my own. I did not *want* to be here doing this now, saying, *"I can't do this. I can't do this without him. I just can't."*

Then I would get angry. I was so angry at Joe for leaving me. I was angry that he left me to do this all on my own. The mixed feelings of anger, loss and emptiness all rolled into one. I didn't know if I wanted to shout or cry.

A lot of people asked me if I would stay in the house, or would I want to move? I didn't even have to give it any thought. No way, he was here. He was absolutely here. His energy was here. There's no way I'd want to leave that behind. Even being in the very place he died was the one place I wanted to be; it was home.

For quite some time though, being outside around the pool area was very hard. It was gut-wrenching. I was just staring at an area that was meant to be family-fun; our family, our fun, but yet all I could do was stare at a still pool.

Without him, it wasn't fun. How could it ever be fun again?

One evening, my family and I were sitting around the dining table. Terri had found some video footage of Joe and Ruby on her phone. We watched it thinking it would be good to see.

But after a few seconds, the tear I felt through my heart was so intense; I remember it just stopped me in my tracks. Dad and Terri were trying to search for more, but I was so torn between wanting to watch, but being so heartbroken by it at the same time. It was an incredibly hard situation to be in and the emotions I had never felt before. Being pulled in so many different ways.

In the end, it was easier not to watch because it felt safer. I wasn't ready to hear his voice, let alone seeing him with Ruby and knowing that could never happen again in her life.

My days were filled with just *getting by*. At first, it was one hour at a time, one cup of tea at a time, one sleep at a time. I would often fall asleep just out of pure exhaustion. My eyes were tired and heavy. My mind, still trying to comprehend what had actually happened. The how's and the why's.

The why's were the hardest.

Why would a young father be taken away from this world? Why would a great man be taken away from this world? Why do all the good ones get taken too soon? The why's never did get answered, not in the early days, anyway.

Donate Life had recommended a local grief counsellor. I made my first appointment a few days in advance. I was quite apprehensive about it as I knew she would ask me all about the death.

Life Goes On

The day came, and she cancelled. I was half relieved but also half so annoyed. I had mentally prepared myself for it.

The following week, the day before my rescheduled appointment, she called again to postpone a second time. I don't know who was angrier; me or my mum! Seriously, as if I needed this to be happening on top?

A few days later, my first counselling session was spent on the floor, having an anxiety attack. I didn't know what was happening to me, but she did. She was very good and obviously had seen this before. I had started to tell her about Joe and what had happened.

And then, I could feel I was shallow breathing. She asked me to lie on the floor. And as I was lying there, feeling like I was going to die from not being able to breathe, she was just casually talking to me.

She put a toy frying pan on my stomach and told me when I breathed in to expand my belly and watch the frying pan lift up.

And as I exhaled, to watch the frying pan go down. This is now what I know as *deep-belly breathing*, but I thought it was bizarre at the time. I remember thinking, *"What is this woman doing? I can't breathe, and she's putting a frying pan on my stomach. What the hell?"*

She was talking away. I wasn't really listening. I was just trying to breathe slowly.

She said to me, *"No one has ever died of a panic attack. You will get through it. You will be absolutely fine."* As I was lying there on the cold floor, I started to shake. I was freezing.

Adrenaline now pumping through my body, as if having a dead husband wasn't enough. The whole hour was spent just breathing until I was able to slowly sit up and then drive home.

My beautiful Dad looked after me so well, too. He thought I could do with better grief support. He booked me in to see a professional

Grief Psychologist in Cottesloe. He drove me there and back to every appointment.

So many anxious thoughts, *"Does she even know that my husband passed away? Do I need to tell her that first? Do I need to go into what exactly happened that morning?"*

I still remember my very first words to her after she asked, *"Tell me about you and Joe."*

I said, "We weren't a lovey-dovey couple… We met in high school…" I continued to say, and the rest is all a blur.

I didn't know why I felt that was important to say, or even why they were the first words out of my mouth, until many years later.

The following two visits were my last. My anxiety from going to the appointments was so high that I was taking Valium when I got home to calm down.

About six weeks had gone by, I decided to go and get my hair done. I booked in with an old hairdresser that I'd seen about a year before. The last time I'd seen her, I was pregnant with Mia, and we didn't know if I was having a boy or the girl at that stage.

As I walked in, we said, hello, and I sat down. She said to me, *"Wow, I haven't seen you in ages. What's been happening?"*

I froze. I got out my phone and showed her a picture of Mia. I said, *"I had a baby girl. I called her Mia."*

She gave her congratulations. And then I just went blank. I couldn't talk. I sat there, wide-eyed and not able to tell her about Joe.

She continued doing my hair. She knew something was wrong, but she obviously wasn't going to pry. Occasionally, she would just touch my shoulder and say, *"Are you okay?"*

Life Goes On

I would just nod. There was no way I could speak. If I had to speak, that would mean not being able to breathe. I just breathed in, out, in, and out. I sat like that for three hours. I could not say a thing. Even as I went to pay and leave, I couldn't say anything. I just waved and gave a half-smile.

Once I got home, I texted my hairdresser. I told her how sorry I was that I couldn't speak. And that Joe had recently passed away. She knew Joe because he had been in there and got his hair cut. She felt so sorry for me. She told me I should have just told her to stop. But I told her I couldn't have even said that, from fear of being out of breath through words.

That was one of my most severe anxiety attacks.

Exhaustion sent me to sleep most nights, but I'd wake up throughout the night, usually early morning. I'd sleep with my blind wide open and stare out at the black sky and the stars. I wondered where he was. That big wide world.

My mind couldn't help but go back to that morning; the visions, the sounds, the shock. I couldn't get the image of him lying there out of my head. Grey-blue lips; thankfully, his eyes were closed. He really did look like he was just sleeping. When I was doing mouth-to-mouth, I could hear the gurgling of the blood inside of his body; his nose bleeding, and the stillness of his body.

I will never forget the sounds of Henry and Ruby screaming, and the image of him lying there, lifeless. The sirens, the commotion, the paramedics. I knew he was dead, but I was somehow expecting a miracle.

Even watching surfers, hearing the sound of the leg rope banging against the surfboard, the smell of the wax, seeing them running towards the beach and jumping into the ocean.

The sight made me feel so empty and miserable. All I wanted to be doing was watching Joe surf - a miracle considering I had spent half my life watching him and watching endless surf videos with him.

The sounds would bring me right back down to grief, sadness and despair. The feelings of unfairness would start all over again.

Then reality would set in. I would see other surfer's girlfriends sitting down the beach, sunbathing and reading; I would be angry. It wasn't their fault, of course, but I was jealous. I was jealous that they got to sit on the beach without a worry in the world, feeling free, relaxing, and enjoying life.

I was not good at expressing my emotions or feelings. I felt very uncomfortable *'letting go'* in front of anyone, and for them to see the real raw me. Most people only saw the shell of me, the outside me. The me that came across okay, that I was coping and doing the best I could. But deep down on the inside, I wasn't doing so well.

Not that I was depressed, but I had a constant struggle of putting on a facade. I needed to show the kids I was still capable. That they had a strong mum that they could rely on.

I was their rock now, so I needed to keep myself in check. The problem was, I kept this facade going almost all the time.

My inner struggles were intense.

The words and messages of *"Amy, you are so strong."*

I hated hearing this!

Because inside, I felt like I was going to burst. Inside I was so fucking wound up with anger, loneliness, and despair that I couldn't believe what people saw in me.

But they saw the shell; they saw me getting up every day; they saw me getting the kids off to school. They saw me *surviving*. Was that strength?

I didn't know what they meant by being strong because I certainly didn't feel it inside.

Life Goes On

I felt like shouting, *"I'm just doing what I have to fucking do... I have to get up and take the kids to school, I have to show up, I have to... I have to... I have to!"*

When all I actually wanted to do was scream, *"I just want my husband back!"*

But ultimately, I did have a choice. I chose to get up every day. I chose to support my children and be the best damn mother and father combined they could ever have.

I only knew my life with Joe. I didn't know how else to do it. There was no manual I could refer to, to give me some direction, some way forward, some explanation of where to go and how to from now.

I also had three very young children. And it came solely down to me to raise them. I was so scared and angry that I *had* to do this.

I didn't sign up for a life on my own with kids. I signed up for marriage and to be with the only man I knew how to be with. I didn't *want* to learn or explore a different way. It was fine, just how it was.

I hated myself for my thoughts sometimes. The only way I felt I could get through 'missing Joe' would be to counterbalance that by focusing on the negative.

I would say to myself, *"He never gave me much attention."* or *"He would rather be surfing, anyway."* or *"He was terrible at looking after me."* or the worst one, *"He was so fucking selfish."*

I couldn't tell anyone I was having these thoughts. It was like a hidden secret that I couldn't reveal. I didn't want to alter people's perception or memory of Joe.

I could only later share these thoughts with my sister-in-law, Hannah.

The loss of Hannah's only brother was extremely difficult for her because they didn't get along at all. Joe didn't understand Hannah, and she didn't understand him. They were chalk and cheese. They fought their whole lives, and even when they were both adults, their views and opinions were the total opposite. Hannah felt that she lived in the shadow of her brother. Joe could do no wrong, and in her eyes, he was the golden child.

We all felt and knew Joe's dad, Nigel, died on the inside that very day Joe died. Very sadly, just five years later, Nigel did pass away. He had no idea he had cancer until one day, he had a stroke. He was in the hospital for three weeks with Julie and Hannah by his side, every single day. The cancer had spread; he was riddled with it. There was nothing that could be done.

My days were filled with *just doing;* I showed up; I took the kids to school; I did the housework. I did whatever needed doing. I talked to people. I had friends over. My family were here. My Mum had organised for me to have a young nanny here three days a week to help me with the kids and household stuff.

Then it was night time.

Every single night for years, Henry cried. It was always at bedtime when everything was quiet, and all the help was gone for the day. Only five years old and the emotions he had to deal with were so unfair.

Tucking him into bed every night, he would cry. He would say, *"Mum, I miss Dad so much. Is he coming back? Why did Dad die? I want him back. It's so unfair, why my Dad?"*

A lump would form in my throat immediately. I cried with him, and said, *"I know it's not fair Henry, I want him back too. I'm so sorry."*

When my mum stayed over, she would often lay with Henry and comfort and reassure him. Kate would also stay over, leaving her two little ones at home with Adam.

Life Goes On

We all made sure Henry, in particular, was given loads of love, cuddles and reassurance.

Knowing how much his heart was breaking and knowing how unfair it was that a five-year-old boy had to go through this; a little boy losing his Dad, absolutely broke me. All I did was curl up with him, hug him tight, tell him we would be okay, that I loved him so much and that I will *always* be there for him.

In reality, I didn't know how I was going to do it. I didn't know how to bring up the kids on my own and if we really would be okay. But I had to reassure him that we would. That it will all be okay. I was also telling this to myself... Somehow, we will be okay.

Ruby was very quiet. I don't know what's worse, hearing your children ask and cry where their Dad is, or not saying anything at all. She called him *"Dadda."* They had a magical bond.

I knew she would've hooked him around her finger when she got older.

I knew he was with her, though. One day, Ruby came out of her bedroom, I was in the kitchen (as usual), she walked straight into the front loungeroom, where she just stared at the photo on the wall, of Joe surfing Roxy's in the Mentawai's.

It was the big print that was taken to the funeral, and where the Mark Twain quote came from. She looked at it for a good few minutes, then casually walked back into her room, without saying anything.

Joe let me know he was around, particularly in the first few months. If you've never experienced the energy of a spirit around, you would be very dubious that this could even happen.

I had never really thought about the possibility of spirits or mediumship. The 'psychic' world is not always taken seriously, and many people don't believe in such things.

SINK or SWIM

I had bought Mia a new toy. It was a big arch that she could eventually crawl through, with bells and other bits hanging off it. In the middle of the arch, it had a door which made a singing noise when it was either opened or closed.

She had just started to play with the toys hanging on the outside, and I showed her how to open and close the door. She loved it when it made the singing noise.

That night, around midnight, I heard a noise. I immediately took more notice as I thought I was dreaming it. Then it happened again:

"Ding, ding, ding!"

Oh, my goodness. It was the music of the opening and closing of the door on the toy.

The only way the noise is made is when the door is pushed open or closed through the middle section. It kept going off, continuously! One after another, with a few seconds in between. I was getting so freaked out. I didn't want to get up because I was scared! I yelled out:

"Joe! If that's you, can you please stop! You're scaring me."

It did it once more, then stopped.

One afternoon, I was lying in my bed, completely exhausted, having a nap. I was half asleep, half awake, in that dreamy state. I could feel and hear someone next to my bed, I felt my covers push down as though someone had very gently sat on my bed. I assumed it was Mum checking up on me and putting a cup of tea on my bedside table.

When I opened my eyes to sit up and drink my tea, nothing was there. I was so confused! I got up and asked Mum if she had come down to check on me, and she said, *"No, I wanted to leave you to sleep."*

Even though I was confused and unsure, I also felt a sense that it was Joe, that he'd come down to check on me.

Life Goes On

My Mum also had an experience a few weeks after Joe passed. She was lying in bed trying to sleep, tossing and turning. After about ten minutes of Eric going to bed, the bedroom TV suddenly turned on.

Mum asked Eric, *"Did you just turn the TV on?"*

He replied, *"No, I thought you did?"*

They were both confused with what was going on. Mum got up and saw that the remote was on the TV bench, nowhere near them. She turned it off and knew instantly; it was Joe.

When she was lying in bed earlier, she was talking to Joe saying how much she missed him, how unfair it all was, and that could he please give her a sign he was listening, and he was around.

Not many people were told about these things happening because until you personally witness it, or it happens to you, it's hard to believe.

Ladybugs are very special and meaningful to the kids and me. After a few short weeks after Joe's death, I was down by the beach, crying my eyes out, looking up at the clouds, wondering where he was, contemplating what *'death'* actually was.

Lots of thoughts were rolling through my head, trying to make some sense of it all. I was starting to hyperventilate, so I rolled over onto my side and there in the grass were about fifteen ladybugs crawling around in the one area. I felt so drawn to them and was in complete awe, watching them scatter around and crawl onto my hands.

From that moment, ladybugs would appear at the most unexpected times. I would be cleaning the pool, and there in the filter box on a leaf, lay three ladybugs. At the time, cleaning the pool was therapeutic, and as always, my thoughts were with Joe.

I would be coming back from a therapy session, and there would be a ladybug on my car door. There have been multiple times where I would be sitting at a café on my own, and a ladybug would come and land on me. There are just too many times to mention how many ladybug visits I have received.

For me, they represent Joe's soul, his presence, his way of saying:

"I'm here, I'm with you."

"Henry has started to sleep in Ruby's bed. He says he wants to protect her. He is so sweet and loving. I think he just needs to be close to Ruby for comfort."
~ Diary Excerpt

CHAPTER 6

Drowning

"If you want happiness, seek happiness within yourself."

Due to my frequent and severe anxiety attacks, my doctor put me on anti-anxiety medication.

I came off them a few times because I felt like I was coping, and that I was okay to not be on medication anymore. Then life would hit me, and I'd go back on them once again.

I had been off them for nearly a year when I travelled to Bali for a little getaway without the kids. I arranged to meet up with a young fireman I had met in Perth, as he was on a surfing trip in Indonesia... And BOOM!

The anxiety hit me like a freight train.

I remember the exact moment it happened.

I was sunbathing on a sun lounger, reading a book, when again, entirely out of nowhere, the dizziness started, the tight chest and the feeling that I couldn't breathe all over again.

"Oh, no! Not now!" I thought. *"I'm meant to be on a relaxing holiday, why the hell am I having an anxiety attack?"*

You see, the minute my body relaxed... BOOM! It hit.

It's like when you go on holidays, mostly you end up sick because you've finally stopped *doing* and rushing around.

I hid it well. But I couldn't eat, and I felt sick the entire time. I still had four days to get through.

My thoughts were on the kids and home. I felt *guilty* for being on holiday. I felt guilty for leaving my family the job of looking after the kids. There's that bloody guilt again. It absolutely ruined my holiday, and all I could think about was wanting to get home.

I saw families wherever I went. Kids in the pool, families dining out together. I had spent a lot of time in Bali with Joe, and it was my first time back without him. It was all too much.

I thought the feeling would cease by the time I got home. But no.

The drive back home was intense. I was trying to hide it from my Dad who picked me up from the airport, but all I could concentrate on was the weird dizzy feeling inside.

I thought maybe once I got home and saw the kids, I would be okay. But no.

I struggled intensely with anxiety for another month before I ended up seeing my doctor and going back on medication. It takes about four weeks for the tablets to start working, so I endured intense amounts of anxiety for two months, before starting to finally feel *'normal'* again.

Anxiety does NOT just go away. I knew exactly what the trigger was, but even after accepting and recognising the anxiety, it was nearly impossible for me to shake it off.

Having intense anxiety all day long, whilst functioning as a mum, being a business owner, doing all the other chores and life's to-do lists, it was utterly so exhausting. You will do anything to stop that feeling. That for me, was taking medication.

I explored other techniques, such as meditation, deep-belly breathing, and EFT tapping. Still, for me, they were just *in-the-moment* techniques that temporarily helped the intensity of the anxiety, but I would still wake up with it every single morning over and over again.

I couldn't go on with it.

Even in the very early days, I had someone comment to me about not needing medication and saying, *"Don't you go on that stuff, you don't need it."*

When my mum found out that this person had said this, she was so angry. She saw how much suffering I had to endure every single day; all she wanted to do was to take it away from me, in any way possible.

From this moment, a seed was planted inside my head that I needed to cope with my trauma and anxiety by not seeking help with medication. That all I needed to do was meditate, breathe, and use essential oils; that would do the trick.

Well. At that stage of my life, I had never meditated, used essential oils or knew anything about any other forms of breathing other than how I *usually* breathe.

I now realise that that was *their* opinion of medication. Perhaps they had not suffered trauma to the extent that I had and was just projecting their opinions and thoughts onto me. At the time, when I was at my lowest, I took on the guilty emotion, by thinking their way was the *right* way.

I could have suffered so much less if I didn't feel guilty that I needed to be strong by not taking medication.

To this day, I am still on medication, and I'm fine with that. Everyone has their own right to their own values, thoughts and opinions. And for me, if I need one little pill to help me function as a widow, a Mum, the sole carer of three kids - two with special needs, a cook, a cleaner, and a domestic goddess all wrapped into one human being, then I will happily take that little pill. Every single day!

Both Henry and Mia have special needs. Henry was diagnosed with permanent hearing loss in both ears at the age of three, then later aged nine, diagnosed with High Functioning Autism. The challenges of Mia's Intellectual Disability didn't really start to appear strongly until the age of five years old. This was like her going through the *terrible two's*, yet she was five.

I had a psychologist and a therapy team through *Disability Service*s. They supported and helped me greatly with lots of visual aids for Mia, but I found I wasn't really getting anywhere with her behaviour at home. The staff changes were challenging as every time a new psychologist started, I had to re-start and explain her needs all over again.

Esta was our first psychologist; she was with us for the first two years. Mia needed more help with fine and gross motor skills and communication, not so much behavioural needs. However, it was Henry who was more challenging for me at this time.

She encouraged me to seek an Autism assessment for Henry.

My life seemed to be all about appointment after appointment for both Mia and Henry.

Drowning

I was often exhausted, and the sheer load of carrying all this without Joe to help and support me was too much.

On this one particular day, I was going through an incredibly hard time with Mia and her behaviour, that I had hit an all-time low.

I rang Kate from Trigg Beach, where I was having my morning coffee. I was due back at the school later in the afternoon as the kids had a running event on. I told her how much I was struggling with Mia, and that I just couldn't cope anymore. Kate was very supportive and knowing that I need practical advice, she told me that she would come over that night and we would go through a plan and schedule together. I kept it together and said thank you and was feeling a little more optimistic about getting some practical help.

But my emotions weren't done with me. I needed to vent and cry; I was feeling so wound up and feeling very sorry for myself. The words again, *"I can't believe I have to do this on my own... It's not fair! Why have I been dealt these fucking hard cards? Not only is my husband dead, but I have special needs children to contend with..."*

I walked over to the groin, where Joe's plaque was and sat down. I felt myself completely let go. All the exhaustion came streaming out. I felt so drained that I had to lay down. The sun was warm on my face, and there was quite a strong breeze from the south, but the rocks were sheltering me.

As I lay there, bawling my eyes out, all I could imagine was walking into the ocean, feeling the cool water on my skin, feeling myself submerge under the water then just swimming out to sea and not coming back. The idea of being 'free' was overwhelming. I just wanted the struggle to stop.

I started hallucinating and saw a man in a white coat staring at me. He had a magnifying glass over his eye and was studying me, saying something like:

"This, ladies and gentlemen, is what you call a mental breakdown."

Then there were other strange people around him, laughing with their faces coming in and out and back and forth.

I heard someone call out, *"Are you okay?"*

I realised a couple had walked up onto the rocks and saw me lying there, curled up in the foetal position. I couldn't see them as they were behind me, and I had no strength to move. I managed to put my hand up and give a slight wave, half hoping they might call someone as I had no energy to even get my phone out of the back pocket of my jeans.

But they took my wave as being okay. I laid there for three hours. I knew I had missed the kids running races. I knew I *had* to get up to get them from school.

It took all my strength to reach back into my jeans pocket and grab my phone. I called my Mum. I could barely talk. I told her to come and get me, that I was on the rocks at Joe's plaque. She was panicked and asked if I had taken anything. I said to her, exhaustingly:

"No, just come and get me. Please."

Heartbreakingly, she saw her daughter in a complete mess. She took my hand and led me back down the rocks to the car, hugging me and telling me she will look after me. I stayed at Mum's for the rest of the afternoon. She called my doctor and came with me to the appointment and explained everything to Maria.

This was the lowest I had been in years. All I wanted was to be checked into a hospital just to *get away* from everything. I didn't want to do life anymore. I didn't want to be strong, I didn't want to be Mum, I didn't want the sole responsibility; I didn't want any more burdens.

I was carrying the weight of my world on my shoulders, with what felt like no one else to help me carry the load. I was completely and utterly exhausted.

Drowning

It's not that I wanted to die; I just wanted to be free from all responsibilities. I wanted someone to look after me for once. I went back to my Psychologist.

I hadn't been in a while because I thought I was on top of things. I mean, I didn't have any major issues, apart from being utterly exhausted from looking after three kids on my own, constant appointments for the kids, behavioural problems, trying to run an interior design business, and looking after the household... I don't know what I was thinking when I thought that I was okay.

I've always been a strong-willed person. I don't believe in *leaning on* others to help. I feel weak when I do so. I'm not sure where that limiting belief came from, but it is something I need to continuously work on.

I organised to stay with a friend down near Mandurah for four days, while Mum moved in and stayed with the kids. She's always been my rock and my biggest support. I am so, so lucky that I have a mum that is so compassionate and understanding of any situation I find myself in. She is always the first one to drop everything and sort it.

"I don't know what will happen in 2 years, or 5 years or even 10 years. But I know that I'm struggling to come to terms that in all of that time, you won't be here to share so many memories that will be made. So many Christmases, Birthday's, and Anniversaries, all of these will be another year away from you."
~ Diary Excerpt

CHAPTER 7

Treading Water

"If you want freedom, free yourself."

After about a year, the fog that I was living in seemed to clear. I could feel myself starting to smile more and laugh more, all while seeing the goodness in things that happened in my world. The kids were growing. I had to adjust to my new life with just the four of us. I started doing things for myself, especially around the house. It had just been renovated just before Joe died. The pool was in, but we had a lot of blank walls.

The first room I decorated was Henry and Ruby's bedroom. They slept together in the same room from a really young age; hence why they have such an amazingly close bond. I didn't like the energy of the room. It was dark and cold. I wanted to give the room a new, fresh light feel.

I hadn't tried any sort of DIY before; but I painted the walls and hung new curtains. I found some old crates on *Gumtree* that I sanded down, varnished, and hung on the wall. I had to learn how to use a drill. Being an old house, the bricks were really soft, so the holes were pretty bad, but it didn't matter because I was learning and did it all myself.

When I stood back, and I'd finished my project, I had the most significant moment of self-satisfaction, I think I'd ever felt in my life. I enjoyed the process so much. It was so therapeutic. It took me away from my grief, and it put me in a place of content and just being in the moment.

It was the first time that I felt I wasn't struggling. My anxiety levels lowered.

I finally found something for me.

In that moment of realising; wow, I finally found my passion. It was a moment of amazement in myself.

Joe and I had always talked about me finding a passion - or at least sticking to something. He had his surfing. That was his number one passion. And I was always really envious of him having that because it was something that he could just do and loved and could get away from the pressures of the world.

I always wanted something like that for myself. But as much as I tried so many things, even as a child, there was nothing that ever stuck. There was nothing I felt I was overly good at. And I didn't really know why I didn't stick at things. If I didn't like it, I just stopped doing it.

But now, finally, I'd found a passion.

But why did Joe have to die for me to find this? That was my next question.

That was my next year of searching for answers. Not as to how or why he died, but more universal thoughts of, okay, so if things happen for a reason, what are the reasons this has happened? Is it because I needed to be independent and find this out for myself? Would I have found this out if Joe hadn't have died?

I wasn't really sure of the answer, but I was willing to find out along the way.

I gradually started to do up the rest of the house. I organised the trades, picked out all the products, even designed the bathroom and laundry renovation. I realised I was using interior designer skills without even having formal training.

So, the next thing on my to-do list was to become an interior designer! I had hope. I had excitement. But even those feelings are a hard thing to have as well, because I would catch myself laughing, enjoying a moment, and then thinking, *"Should I be having this much enjoyment?"*

And then the dreaded guilt would set in.

A school friend of mine put me in touch with an incredible holistic counsellor. I saw Gemma on and off for quite a few years, and she really helped me put so many things into perspective. I realised for me this type of counselling was what I needed. The traditional talk therapy of a psychologist at the time was too confronting. And I didn't find it actually really helped me. I needed real, purposeful things to focus on and *do* - not just talk.

Gemma really did help me turn my life around. I had so many 'ah-ha' moments! I realised I had been given a second chance to live my life to the fullest. And it was by no means putting Joe down or even putting my life with him down. It was more turning it around and making the most of what I have now, what my new normal looks like, and how to move forward and enjoy my life with my children.

It was never about moving on. You can never *move on*. Anyone that is grieving understands and knows this. And it's something we don't talk about much in society.

When people say, *"Oh, it's been a few years. She should move on..."* It cuts deep.

It's a very, very hurtful thing to say because it's almost like they're telling you to forget about the person that you have loved and spent your entire life with and to just get on with it. They may not mean it that way, but that is how it is received.

That is why we, the grieving, who have lost someone, will always say we are *moving forward*. Forward in a way that we can enjoy our lives, love those that are around us, and know and understand that the ones we have lost, would want this for us. Wholeheartedly.

And if it was the other way around and you were looking down on your partner, you would want them to live their best life.

So, that is the path that I chose.

I chose happiness over sadness.

I chose to honour Joe in everything that I did.

I chose for him to be proud of me, the new me, my new passions, my new paths in life, my ability to learn and grow and find new meaning in life.

I chose to enjoy what I've been given with the kids and my family. Living a simple, happy life, but also filled with purpose and desire, love, honesty, content, and passion.

I still had moments of anxiety and emotional breakdowns. The down moments hit pretty hard, and I've found myself constantly feeling stuck again and again. That feeling of constantly climbing over mountains to get anywhere.

There are many struggles. There are moments that I'm just so sick of being alone and doing it all by myself. Especially the challenges with the kids. Having that sole responsibility on my shoulders can sometimes be too much to bear.

The thing I miss the most – being in love and having someone (a partner) love me. I forget how it feels to have someone so meaningful in your life. Someone to walk alongside with and do life together. I feel terribly alone at times.

Every evening while the kids were in bed, I'd just sit up by myself, watch TV and be alone. I didn't have the husband time where I could unwind from my day and listen to my husband's day.

Sure, I could have called someone - but I was also exhausted. And it was just so much easier to sit and watch TV and just zone out because my brain was always switched on.

The only moments where I felt peace was when I was asleep.

Every waking moment, my brain was on. And it was on in a million places at once. It was on in the past. It was on in the present. It was on in the future. It was on about me, about the kids. It was just constantly on, and there was no break from it.

I needed something for me, an outlet to enjoy and focus on, and declutter my brain.

After realising I had quite a knack for interior design, I decided I would study it. I looked around online and found a *Diploma of Interior Design and Decoration*. I thought, *"Yep, that's it. I'm going to do it. This is what I want to do with my life. I'm going to become an interior designer!"*

I was *so* excited.

Finally, I had hope. I had excitement, and I had a passion, and I couldn't wait to start studying and getting stuck into it.

SINK or SWIM

The diploma course was two and a half years long. I studied every day. The kids were at school and Mia in day care. As soon as I finished my diploma, I started my own business. It was such an exciting time. Finally, I was doing what I loved. I'd spent a lot of time and effort into studying, and it was paying off. I was really excited to be on this new journey.

Two years after losing the love of my life, a very special person came into my life by answering a *Gumtree* ad that I'd put on for a nanny.

Kobie answered the ad, and we had a quick chat. As soon as she came to the door, I just knew she was for us. She had her own family, two kids and a husband who is a builder. She was able to dedicate time to my kids and me by working for us as a nanny and even more importantly, becoming a beautiful, good friend to me.

I believe the universe had something to do with this one.

Kobie pretty much became my house husband. She saw me at a lot of different times that other people didn't, including my family. She saw me at the end of the day when I had nothing else to give. I'd plunk myself down on the couch, totally mentally exhausted. And there she was bringing me my dinner and making me cups of tea.

I've always kept my emotions to myself. It's not that I bottle them up or sweep them under the carpet. Far from it, actually. I let them out, but I let them out when I'm on my own, in my own time. I recognise when I'm feeling sad, angry or flat. I don't often admit to people that I'd spent half the night crying because, by the next day, I'm okay.

Many nights I would stay up quite late into the night by myself and look at old photo albums, listen to music, songs that reminded me of Joe or our past life travelling and being together. I enjoyed reminiscing on my own. I found I could connect with Joe better that way. And it was my time.

It was *my time* to grieve in *my way*.

Treading Water

Some bittersweet news was received after Joe's passing. Following his wishes, he was able to donate his corneas and bone tissue. The first recipient was a young boy in his early teens who suffered from a condition called Keratoconus. It's a degenerative disorder of the cornea. The second recipient was a woman in her 50's who suffered from a condition called Fuchs' Dystrophy, which causes pain and swelling to the cornea and impaired her vision.

It was a very heart-warming and proud moment that he was able to provide a better life to those who needed it.

After reflecting on the person Joe was, I remember a conversation I had with Kate. I asked her, *"What do you think Joe saw in me? What was it about me that he loved, do you think?"*

She answered with something I never really thought about, *"Joe needed you, as much as you needed him. You were his calm to his chaos."*

I was questioning my self-worth. Joe was such a character, full of charisma, life, motivation... I really wondered what it was about *me* specifically, that Joe loved. I really did not know.

But, eventually, I did.

One of the scariest things I ever did was step into the unknown world of dating. About a year and a half had gone by, and I was really missing affection, and someone to talk to; male company. I really missed it. As much as I still talked to Joe every day, and I'd write him letters, I needed the physical presence. I'd never ever been with anyone else.

Joe was all I knew from the age of 16. So, it was a huge step for me.

I had a few short-term relationships, ranging from lasting a few weeks to the longest being eighteen months. Even though they didn't work out, every one of them taught me something new. I was learning to discover what attributes and qualities were important to me. Some offered a lot of affection, which at first, I loved and felt like I was in love all over again.

But then, I needed more. I needed connection, I needed deep and meaningful conversations, I needed fun and laughter, I needed positivity and a carefree, relaxed vibe. Mostly, I discovered these men had a lot of jealousy, anger, and mistrust.

The one that lasted eighteen months wasn't a traditional relationship. It was an *'after hours'* delight. The attraction and chemistry with a very good looking, young firefighter was something I had never encountered before. He was ten years my junior, but that didn't bother either of us.

It worked because we became best friends. We talked every day. We talked shit. We had deep and meaningful conversations, all while drinking too much red wine.

But it was what I needed at the time.

It was *'no strings attached'*; there was no pressure or expectations, but he did keep showing up at my doorstep most weekends.

I did feel shame and guilt for being with another man. But, I felt it was my time to enjoy for myself. There were no nappies to change, there was no nagging, there were no to-do lists. It was just simply enjoying the company and the moment.

He really was a big part of my journey, though. He made me realise that what I was doing, and what I had been through was truly unique.

He was my biggest cheerleader at the time. He gave me encouragement and support, laughter and fun. He taught me to laugh again. He taught me I was desirable and sexy. He always made time for me and always had a smile - and some good, wholesome energy that lifted me up. That was one of the reasons why I enjoyed being around him.

Treading Water

He was young, carefree, and easy on the eye. All of my troubles and frustrations with the kids, and life, or whatever else was going on, just melted away when he was around. He appreciated me for who I was. He truly made me feel like I was someone significant and worthy.

I'll never forget how he made me grow, helped me to become more self-assured, self-confident, and to find some inner happiness. I found my laughter and joy, and for that, I'll be forever grateful to him.

Eventually, as all good things do, it had to come to an end - for me to move forward in my life.

Plus, if I didn't move him on, he would've just kept on showing up at my door.

I was a woman on a mission to keep enhancing my life.

"I've had a very low couple of days. I miss you soooooo much that I nearly can't bear it. I just want you back. I had a dream last night that I was holding your hand, and it felt so nice. I miss your touch, I miss your hugs, your chest, your arms, your hands, your laugh lines, your energy, your presence, your voice, your laugh, our conversations. So much gone."
~ Diary Excerpt

CHAPTER 8

Through A Widow's Window

*"If you want sunshine and lollipops,
find your inner sweetness."*

One of the biggest challenges I faced was; do I continue to wear my wedding ring and how long for?

It had been about 18 months. Something stopped me in my tracks when I thought about wedding vows. I was still wearing my wedding ring, and I still felt I have - or had - a husband, but then I remembered: *"Til' <u>death</u> do us part."*

I remember thinking *"Oh God. Does that mean the contract is null and void? Does that mean I'm actually not married?"*

And that was correct. I was officially not married. Joe will always be my husband in my heart, but it was a really strange feeling and concept to comprehend. I felt so empty and sad.

I felt sad because this was not what I'd signed up for. I didn't want to be an 'only' parent. The stigma that comes with being single. I hated it. I hated explaining to strangers that I was a *single parent*.

There was always that automatic feeling of not being good enough, or that I'm simply unwanted goods. I didn't want strangers knowing my business, but then I also didn't want them to assume my husband had purposefully left me.

It would inevitably come up in conversation about my husband. Questions such as, *"Where's your husband?"* or *"What does your husband do?"*

I always had to decide on the spot what I would respond with. I would take a deep breath and prepare myself mentally (all within seconds) and generally respond with, *"He actually passed away."*

It tended to be a conversation stopper.

Not many people know what to do with that. What do they say? Mostly, *"Oh, I'm sorry to hear that."*

Then I feel like I need to explain more because they are looking awkward. I don't want people to feel awkward around me.

Sometimes I'll just respond with *"Thank you."* and leave it at that. But then sometimes I get asked, *"How did he die?"*

Sigh.

I really didn't want to go into it as it's a place that's hard to go. I learned to *tell the story* without any emotion. Just state the facts. But then I'd get asked more questions, and hear more statements like, *"Wow, he was so young. Did he have a bad heart? Was he sick?"*

Through A Widow's Window

I know people want to know, but it is so hard whilst trying to be social to talk about such deep, tragic moments, that pull me away from a light, carefree conversation.

I just didn't want to explain it anymore. I was really tired of being the widow and explaining it and identifying with it.

Then there was the filling in of the forms. Title of Ms, Mrs, Miss... What am I? Marital status. Married, single, or separated? Well, I'm not any of those. Very rarely do forms have *widowed* as an option. It makes you feel alienated; that you don't fit into a box. It makes it even more real, and more pertinent.

In the very early days, I wanted people to know he died. I wanted them to know what I'd just been through, and I guess, share with me in the disbelief.

As time went on, I didn't want anyone to know, or I wanted to almost hide it. I didn't want it to define me. I didn't want to be the girl that lost her husband. I just wanted to be Amy, and that was it.

But I felt like I just carried this sign with me and my only identity, was of being a widow. The girl that lost her husband. Looking back, I believe it was my own awareness, my own insecurity or anxiety about it.

I did everything I could to keep Joe's memory alive. I don't know if I was doing it for me or the kids, his mates or his family, but it was just something that I felt I had to do. I felt so strongly that I needed to keep him alive somehow. I didn't want people to stop talking about him or for him to become a faded memory; because for me, I lived with it every single day.

I was envious that other people could have a break from it, that they could just go back to their lives and take a break. They could perhaps not think about Joe for a few days, a few weeks, or maybe even a few months. But for me, it was constant. There was no break, so I felt like I wanted to keep sharing it.

SINK or SWIM

For the first few years, I organised celebrations of Joe's life on the anniversary of his death. We would meet down at Trigg Beach; the beach where we got married ten years prior, the beach where his plaque rests upon the rocks, and the beach where the kids and I scattered some of his ashes.

With a good turnout of friends and family, we would meet there before sunset. I'd give out helium balloons to everyone, and we would write our own messages on the balloon and send it up into the sky, right on sunset.

For me, it was the most honourable thing I could have done for him. I did it for everyone; so we could all come together. I did it, so I knew at least this one day, everyone was thinking about Joe. That's what I wanted for him because he deserved it. He deserved our thoughts and our love. It was hard for me to do, but it was like the eulogy at the funeral. I felt so strongly that I knew I had to do this.

Obviously now, sending plastic up into the sky is not the best idea. We did it for three years before I realised the time had come where I had to let go of that ceremony, and that I had to be okay with everyone thinking about Joe whenever they did and not needing a day to bring everyone together.

Then there were the school holidays. I didn't want my kids to miss out on camping and a life that they would have had if Joe was here. Sitting around a campfire, being in tents, and stargazing. So, being the Miss Independent I was (and firmly are, now), I took them on my own.

For a couple of years, I took them down to Margaret River, three hours south of Perth, just the four of us. We'd stay in a safari tent, we'd light a fire – although I generally didn't actually light them, there were communal fires, and we sat around them. We found sticks for toasting marshmallows. We cuddled up in bed and watched movies on an iPad. The kids had torches, and they would giggle at night in the tent. There was the midnight going-to-the-toilet, waking me up constantly, *"Mum, I can't find my shoes! Mum, I need the toilet. Mum, Mum, Mum!"*

Through A Widow's Window

It was all on me, but I wanted to be with them. I wanted that special time, and I wanted them to know that we can do this as a family, the four of us. Mum can take them camping. Mum can do a lot of things, and I was not going to let them miss out on family camping holidays just because they don't have a Dad.

One particular night, it was the night before we were about to leave. I headed over to a group of people standing by a communal fire, and I asked them if they would like my firewood because I was leaving the next day. We were just having a chat when one of the guys said to me, *"Oh, so are you here on your own?"*

I replied, *"Yeah, yeah. I just brought the kids down."* He responds with, *"Oh, well, where's Dad?"* I rolled my eyes and thought, *"Oh, here we go, again..."*

I said, *"Well, he actually passed away."*

He said, *"Oh shit. Jeez, mate. So fucking sorry, hey? Wow. So, you're down here on your own, doing this on your own?"*

I said, *"Yeah."*

He said, *"Hats off to you. That is amazing."*

I was a little bit taken aback, but I was actually really thankful. I said to him, *"Oh, cheers. Yeah, you know, I don't want them to miss out so, I can do it."*

He said, *"That's the attitude, love. Good on you, hey? You must be really proud of yourself."*

And I was.

In that moment, standing around by the fire, watching my kids happily eat their marshmallows. I stood there, and I thought, *"Yeah, I CAN do this. I am pretty fucking amazing, aren't I?"*

It's nice to be acknowledged. It's nice when people recognise the small things that you do, who you are. I felt really proud in that moment.

It's all the small things I miss, though. No one to look after me when I'm sick, put the bins out, open a tight lid, cook me a meal, tell me they love me, talk to at the end of the day, cuddle up with on the couch, bed snuggles, all the physical touch - gone. All the special gestures - gone. Bedtime routine on my own, night after night...

No guidance on decisions, feeling the weight of the world, solely on me, being entirely depended on by three little humans who all want to share my love equally. And being on-call, all the time. 24/7.

There is no one to take over in the moment if I'm having a bad day.

It's easy to get caught up in these little things I miss out on. I have plenty of days when this is all I feel. Alone. Fed up. Exhausted.

That same thought pattern comes back, *"I did not sign up for this. I hate doing this by myself. It's not fair!"*

But there is nothing I can do about it. It's okay to have days like this.

I give myself permission to feel these emotions because I can't be *Super Woman* all the time. I don't have to be strong and amazing every single day.

Henry with his message for Dad

Ruby with her message for Dad

Mia and her balloons for Dad

Casey, Jol, Brad, Amy, Russell, Clayton & Mike

My message – Always in your Honour

"I feel like everyone thinks I'm doing okay, that I'm over it and moving on. Just because they see me smile, laugh, 'being happy' and just getting on with things. I hate this conflict of emotions."
~ Diary Excerpt

CHAPTER 9

Dreaming Underwater

"**YOU** were the pillar of hope when you were born."

I was standing on the sandy bottom of the deep ocean floor. I had chains around my wrists. I looked around, and I saw Joe standing on my left. He also had chains around his wrists, but he wasn't struggling. He was just standing there, looking so peaceful. As I looked around, there was another figure standing on my right, but I couldn't make out who it was. I knew I had to get the chains off to get to the surface. I started fiddling with the chains, as they came off, they fell heavily to the ocean floor. I looked at Joe, and he smiled at me and nodded for me to go up. So, naturally, I swam to the surface.

As I took my first deep breath, I felt relieved. I swam to the shallows. I looked back down into the crystal-clear water and realised Joe was still down there; I could see him clearly. But there was no movement. He didn't even try to unshackle himself. Nor swim for the surface. He was still and motionless. I realised instantly; he had drowned.

The morning I woke up after this dream, turned out to be one of the most extraordinary, memorable days throughout my journey of grief.

Kate had come over early in the morning. She was sitting on the end of my bed, and I was telling her about my dream.

I didn't realise the significance of it until I was voicing it aloud. As I told her about it, tears welled up, a big lump formed in my throat as I tried to fight back the tears.

It was then she said, *"Well, maybe the other figure, was you? A part of you will always be with him."*

It hit me deep in my heart. My chest felt heavy and sad. I knew at that exact moment that I had to do this on my own. That a part of me would always stay with Joe, but the other part had to leave. I had to rise to the surface to survive; to become me.

I had to swim.

Little did I know, my sister had sent a special message out to my close friends and family the night before, and she had named the event, *"Make Amy Smile Day."*

After asking Kate what made her do this, she replied with:

"I sent out a message saying how Amy really needed to hear how amazing she was. Amy was doing well, but the constant day-to-day reminders were really hard. Everyone had started to get on with their lives. They were booking their holidays away. It was coming up to Amy's third Christmas without Joe, and it was never an easy time. I really felt for Amy still suffering from such deep grief but showing up every day. We were all still there looking after her and the kids, but the inner struggles she hid well."

Dreaming Underwater

That day, I received a constant flow of beautiful, encouraging and thoughtful messages, gifts, phone calls, flowers, and cards. You name it, I got it.

Tears were shed. Hugs were given. Heartfelt love was truly felt.

That day was the day I realised I could do this.

I remembered our pact we had many years ago, and that we had talked about how we would want to die together, when the time came. How uncanny it was, that I was to dream about us being shackled together under the ocean together, just as we'd imagined it would be.

Only, I broke free and swam for the surface. He was right beside me, telling me to swim.

And swim I did.

"You always said I had good intuition, but I never saw this coming. I always thought I would know if something was going to happened to you. I thought I would FEEL it by having a knowing that something wasn't right."
~ Diary Excerpt

CHAPTER 10

Rising Above

"YOU were that miracle that grew inside your mother's womb."

Not only did I have to learn a new way of living without my husband, but I also had to learn how to be on my own and become my own person. Growing up with Joe was so easy; it was simple. We made decisions together, but more often than not, I was happy to go along with what he wanted to do. He'd shown me the world, and we'd travelled to so many places, and without him, I wouldn't have done any of that. I am forever grateful for that, and I'll always cherish those memories.

However, what I had to do next was learn: *Who is Amy?*

It's always been *Joe and Amy.* I had to step out from under his umbrella and become my own person.

It was pretty tough to do so, especially whilst in the midst of grief, loneliness, anger, frustration, hurt, and my personal favourite, guilt.

My first self-discovery was interior design; realising that I could do all these things around the house. I had to learn, but I enjoyed it, and I knew I could do it. I didn't need a man to do all these things. I enjoyed being out in the garden and doing the gardening – that Joe used to do.

I started to be really proud of what I could do.

I started to listen to different types of music that I found I liked. I started to question what my opinions and thoughts were about certain topics. I discovered clothes! And nice ones, not just Kmart or Target brands.

I was never a 'girly girl' who wore makeup or false nails. I prided myself on being a 'low maintenance' wife. I never bought magazines, or handbags, or jewellery. I never treated myself to facials or massages. What a daggy mum I was! But, *self-love* and having nice things that made me feel good wasn't even considered.

It took me quite some time to adjust making sole decisions. After twenty years of always discussing things before you buy, or just going without because money is best spent on the mortgage, I would often second guess myself or try to think what Joe would say or want to do. I even found myself replying to people or making comments that I felt Joe would have said.

I really found it difficult to separate from *Joe and Amy* to being just *Amy*.

But over time, I learned the skill of self-reflection. Maybe that's why I feel I need a lot of time and space to myself. I am slow to process information and find I need that time to seek clarity and work it out in my head by having a good feeling and understanding of what I think and feel about a particular situation or event, before outwardly expressing myself.

It's amazing when we sit in silence, what comes to us. I love just being in a quiet room or sitting outside, in nature, somewhere where I can close my eyes and just stop, have space and let all the busy thoughts just melt away. Then there is room for anything else that needs to come to the surface.

I find these moments provide me clarity, recognition and learning. By allowing these moments of stillness, so much information about ourselves can unfold right before our eyes. I can feel how busy my brain is when I stop. I imagine it like my head is full of rocks, and as I lie down in my quiet space, I feel all the rocks dropping down, out of my head, clearing out the way and allowing that free space to flow in my mind.

It feels very liberating. In the quiet, you can hear many things, important things that really matter.

This is how my book came to me. In a quiet space I held for myself, I saw an image of a book. The first words I saw were, *"I always knew I would marry him."*

After that moment, I knew I would write a book about my journey. And it didn't matter whether it was a top seller or if anyone read it. It was more something I felt in myself that I had to do – and wanted to do. Confirmation that I needed to share my story; my inspirations and life challenges to hopefully help those that may be going through something similar.

Most of all, I found space and quietness. And that's one thing I would like to share – to not take the quiet time for granted.

You learn more in ten minutes of silence than you do in a whole day of thinking.

I owe my personal growth to making mistakes. I've made a lot of mistakes. I've made financial mistakes, and of course, I've made a few, wrong personal decisions – here or there. Sometimes, I haven't said what I should have said or what I wanted to say. But that's how I've grown and learned about me, and who I am as a person.

I realise I have a lot of love in me to give. I'm passionate, creative, and I need an outlet for that. So, when faced with *just being Mum*, I struggled.

I really struggled *just* doing that. And by *just*, I don't mean it's unworthy. Far from it, actually.

It is the hardest (yet most rewarding) job in the world, being a parent.

Unfortunately, though, it's sometimes taken for granted. When I was asked the question *"So, what do you do?"* Before I had my own interior design business, I would reply with *"Oh, I'm a Mum."* And it felt like the conversation ended right there.

I struggled with just being Mum because I needed that creative outlet. I needed something for me, something that would fill up my heart cup. And don't get me wrong, my children do help fill up my heart cup, but they can also be the biggest drainers!

One of my biggest lessons is to absolutely trust my intuition; my gut. It has served me well over and over again. And it's something that'll always be my go-to.

If I'm not sure about something I will stop, and I will ask myself, how do I feel inside about this decision I'm making? The answer is usually there, somewhere inside. I've always had a relatively strong intuition. Joe was always quite amazed by it. And he *always* trusted it.

I began to learn that only I am responsible for myself. I am responsible for my own thoughts, my own actions, my own words, and my own reactions. It was also up to me as to how I wanted to *feel* in that moment, in a day, in an hour, in a week; I don't like to feel down and miserable. It's not me. I don't feel it's fair to bring negative energy onto other people. I am naturally a happy, positive person. I love to spread joy and good vibes because every single person deserves to feel that way.

One of the biggest things that has helped me in moments of self-doubting negative talk is bringing that BFF Amy next to me, the one that would be a true best friend to someone. I feel her put her arm around me. And I imagine what she would say. Wow, such positivity, such kind words. And that's me talking to me; instantly, you feel better.

Rising Above

Snap yourself out of the little mood or the moment you were stressing over or having anxiety about. Sometimes, in the grand scheme of things, it's really not worth it. Just take a few deep, big breaths and either act on it – or let it go. One of my favourite quotes is:

"If it's out of your hands, it deserves freedom from your mind too." (Ivan Nuru)

If there is absolutely nothing you can do about a situation, the best thing you can do for yourself is to free it from your mind. And that doesn't mean sweeping it under the carpet and forgetting about it, it just means putting it in a box or a bubble and leaving it there for the time being. Until you're ready to deal with it, to work on it, or perhaps, in the end, burn it and let it go.

Another great insight that I've learned is when you get triggered by something that someone has said, and you get angry – it just means they have pushed your button. There is something within you that has risen up and doesn't like what they've said. Either it's true, or it's stuff you haven't dealt with.

It could be a story that you're telling yourself about a situation, or it might be a time when you were younger; something happened, and it made you feel a similar way. The same reaction is coming up.

So, the next time when someone says something to you, and you get triggered: Stop. Let the conversation go.

In your own time, go back to that conversation and ask yourself these questions.

How did I feel when they said that? Why did I feel it? Where is this coming from? Have they made me feel unworthy? Have they made me feel unlovable?

And if the answer is *yes* to the last two, then it's not really *them* making you feel that way. It's yourself feeling that way.

SINK or SWIM

As soon as we step up and become accountable, for our own thoughts, feelings, and opinions, the blame game stops. Relationships get better; friendships get better. And you know what?

Your heart and your inner soul will feel better. You will feel like a better person that treats people with respect and honesty.

There were so many things I had to learn about having my daughter, Mia. That included patience and love. Two things that I've found quite challenging to give.

And by love, I don't mean the unconditional-you're-my-daughter-type-of-love. I mean, showing love when you're angry, showing love when you are at your wit's end, and you just don't know what to do anymore. That is extremely hard to do. But it was something that I had to learn and continue to learn because of her disability.

Mia was diagnosed with GDD, Global Developmental Delay, when she was just three years old. She then got retested at the age of seven, and her development had not improved much, so she was deemed to have Intellectual Disability.

Mia requires a different type of parenting to Henry and Ruby. It's hard switching from something that you know has worked twice over. Showing love and compassion for Mia when she's having a meltdown, when she's kicking, screaming and biting me; that takes strength.

That takes a whole lot of courage, resilience, and patience. That requires a profound amount of compassion, usually when I have nothing left to give.

It helps seeing things from her perspective, trying to see how she is feeling and what she is going through in that moment. Putting myself in her shoes at her young age and trying to understand what is going on for her. What emotions does she feel that she is unable to communicate? Like most of us could have felt at that young age.

Rising Above

At the end of the day, love, hugs, compassion and understanding is what works. It usually stops the meltdown in its tracks. Mostly, that is all she needs. Sounds easy, right? Hah.

I have an amazing bond with my children. We are all very close. We share lots of love and moments together. I depend on them as much as they depend on me. We do things for each other. They help me out around the house. I've brought them up to be respectful and understanding. Henry and Ruby have grown up with Mia's developmental issues, which is very challenging. But that will make them even more resilient as teens and adults. It will make them compassionate and understanding of different people's needs and the different reactions required.

But I also have many fears that I need to face on my own. My fears are that I can't give myself three ways. It's very hard to give one-on-one attention to each child. And they all need me – and my time. I try to do all that I can.

We enjoy each other's company, and they enjoy their independent time, too, as much as me. We all work really well together. And I feel so protective of them and of our bond. I don't want to let anything get in the way of that because it's very, very special.

I have fears of getting it wrong. It's solely on me to bring up a teenage boy now. What if I don't guide him in the best way? What if not having a dad negatively affects him through his teenage years? I don't know how it's going to affect him. But what I can do, is be there for him as his mum, give him love, guidance, and support.

I will always try my best to really understand my children, communicate with them, love them for who they are and be the best mother they could ever have.

"I can picture your face as if you were here, telling me what happened to you, shaking your head with tears in your eyes with pure disbelief. I hope you weren't calling for me. I hope it wasn't painful, I hope it was quick."
~ Diary Excerpt

CHAPTER 11
Embracing Emotions

"And **YOU** are still that miracle."

I allow myself to cry.

I allow myself to feel sad.

I allow myself to feel angry.

I allow myself to feel joy and happiness.

I allow myself to feel sorry for myself.

I allow myself to have moments of weakness.

I allow myself fun and laughter and good times.

SINK or SWIM

I allow myself memories.

I allow myself to be frustrated.

I allow myself to be hurt.

I allow myself to feel lonely.

I allow myself time to do nothing and enjoy it.

When you allow yourself all of these things, all of these emotions, all of these feelings, you become *in flow* with life.

I think about other people and what they are going through. In comparison to some, I'm rich. And I don't mean money-rich. I mean, life-rich.

I have a beautiful home designed by my beautiful husband. I had twenty incredible years of life with my husband. Travel, laughter, fun, and exploring. I have three beautiful, exceptional children that light my day up every single day. I have a beautiful, caring, supportive family, always there for one another. So yes, in comparison, I *am* rich.

In moments of my despair or sorrow, in times when I feel down, and life really isn't fair, I think about others. I think about those parents that are sitting in a hospital, watching their precious children go through chemo or operations; or maybe they're just constantly sick in and out of the hospital. Can you imagine what their life feels like?

I have happy, healthy children that I am so grateful for.

There are so many situations that you can think about where others are worse off. And what does that do for me? It puts things into perspective.

Yes, I have a hard life sometimes. I get angry. I get frustrated. I get sad. I cry. I get hurt. I've been used a few times, but I get up the next day, and I keep going because tomorrow is a brand-new day. It's a day to start over.

Embracing Emotions

I feel so much happier and in the flow of life when I just allow. I allow all those emotions just to be there; I acknowledge them, and I accept them. And it's okay to feel every single one of them. I like to sit with them, and eventually, it doesn't seem as hard to carry on once you've acknowledged and just allowed them in. It's like you're just riding the wave and going with the flow. It's *so* much easier than pushing against it. Just sit down and ride it.

So, what kept me going?

The simple answer: My kids. I had to show up for them every day. For years, I used to say, *"I have no choice but to show up."*

But in actual fact, I did have a choice. I could've not got up. I could've let other people take care of things for me and not be involved. I could've turned to alcohol and drugs. I could've stayed in a hole and not come out. But I *did* make a choice. I chose to show up every day. I chose to be there for my kids every day. I chose to be their rock.

I chose them.

It is them who have shown me love. It is them that have given me my unconditional love. Knowing that I am their all, I am their life, I am their mum, their superhero, their number one love... *That* is what gives me my strength, my determination, and my courage to show up.

Every single day.

At first, the most immense burden was the kids. As sad as that sounds, it was the honest truth. How could I possibly look after their needs, while I had absolutely nothing to give? I had nothing left to give; I was an empty cup.

Every time I looked at them, I felt sick, the hole in my heart got bigger and deepened until all I felt was a massive void inside me. But, I still chose to show up for them.

"It seems everyone is just getting on with their lives. I'm not angry nor blaming anyone, but I wished they realised how much this affects me every single fucking day. I can't escape it. I wish I could sometimes. I wish I could just pack up and go on holiday and have a fucking fun time. But I can't."
~ Diary Excerpt

CHAPTER 12

Inspired To Swim

Fast forward to seven years after Joe's death.

Here I am writing my first book! And about to embark on studying a Bachelor of Art Therapy.

I knew this was the path for me when I discovered Art Therapy whilst looking for something new to study. I love helping others. I have been through grief, trauma and loss. I have two children with special needs. I have been through many different types of therapy myself and wished I had found something like Art Therapy when I was grieving.

I will continue to love Interior Design, but my heart yearns for more. Yearning for more of a deeper connection and a greater sense of purpose.

I know I'm here for a magical purpose. I can feel it. I know Joe's death was meant to happen FOR me to be where I am today, and where I am heading for my future.

When I think back to all those years ago, when I asked Kate; *"What do you think Joe saw in me?"*

SINK or SWIM

I now know.

Because *this* is what I see:

I am courageous.

I am inspirational.

I am strength.

I am real.

I am vulnerable.

I am passionate.

I am fun.

I am honest.

I am creative.

I am kind.

I am positive.

I am determined.

I am spontaneous.

I am open.

I am love.

I am Amy Williams.

My challenge to you is: What do you see in YOU?

Conclusion

"I have stepped up to the plate, like a warrior fighting in honour."

In honour of my husband.

In honour of our twenty years of life together.

In honour of myself.

In honour of my children.

In honour of my life.

I choose to be here.

I am ready to face whatever is going to come my way.

Afterward

The encouragement and support my family have given me over the years has been nothing short of amazing. Not only have they had to help me, but they have had to deal with their own grief, as well.

My father and mother-in-law lost their son.
My sister-in-law lost her brother.
My Mum and Dad lost their son-in-law.
My sister lost her brother-in-law.

Joe meant so much to all of us. He was in my family for twenty years. A lifetime of memories made. They saw Joe and I grow up together. They saw us blossom into a family. They were there, every single step of the way.

They had to witness me, their daughter, sister, and in-laws, go through insurmountable pain and suffering. I cannot imagine how hard that would have been for them.

My Dad would say with tears in his eyes, *"I just wish I could fix it for you, honey."*

SINK or SWIM

No one knew what to do, or how to do it, because we had never been there before. None of us had been in this situation before.

One thing I know now is everyone grieves differently, and at different times. There is no right or wrong way to grieve. We generally stumble our way through it, not knowing how to do it, what to do, how to feel, or what to do about those feelings.

It is the unknown.

Until...

You *have* been through it.
You *have* survived it.
You *have* somehow come out the other end and seen the light once again.

Acknowledgments

I would like to acknowledge and give my thanks, love and gratitude to EVERYONE who has been there for me during my rollercoaster journey (and continues to be there!)

With special thanks to:

My Mum, Christine, my Dad, Cliff and my sister, Kate. I love you all so much. We will be forever bonded as our special, little family. Thank you for everything you do for my little family and me.

My mother-in-law, Julie, my sister-in-law, Hannah and always remembering my late father-in-law, Nigel.

My special extended family, Terri, Eric and Adam.

All of my other extended family.

All of my very close friends: You know who you are. I love you all so much and I am so blessed to have you in my life.

SINK or SWIM

All of my high school LJBC friends and School-Mum's, and all of Joe's surfing mates, wives and partners.

Plus, everyone else who has touched my life in some way.

Also, to these special people that I have mentioned in my book, and/or Grief Survival Guide, who have helped me on my journey:

Gemma Colquhoun – Holistic Counsellor - Perth, WA
Antonia Pizzata – Healer - Facebook: Antonia's Sanctuary - Perth WA
Adam Hansen – NLP – www.ahfhealthandfitness.com.au - Perth, WA
Cliff Rollins – Medium – Facebook: Do Divine Oneness - Perth, WA
Simplicity Funerals – www.simplicityfunerals.com.au - Perth, WA

My personal story and my grief survival guide offer my help, advice and techniques on what I discovered along the way. I am not a professional psychologist nor a therapist. Please always seek professional help if you are not coping. The following networks in Australia are available to help:

The Grief Centre of WA – www.griefcentrewa.org.au
Beyond Blue – www.beyondblue.org.au
Griefline – www.griefline.org.au
Health Direct – www.healthdirect.gov.au

The Grief Survival Guide

Introduction

Have you been through grief, trauma and loss?

Do you need inspiration and motivation to *live your best life* after grieving?

Do you know someone who is going through grief and needs some guidance?

Do you want to learn about resilience, growth, strength and living a life of love and freedom after grief?

Do you want to learn how to have your own self-discovery journey?

The Grief Survival Guide came together as I was writing my personal story. I quickly realised along the way that I had a lot to offer in terms of advice, support, encouragement and inspiration.

This guide is not only for those going through grief, but for anyone who is supporting those going through these tumultuous times.

SINK or SWIM

I have created templates that you can print out and fill in. You will find all the templates in the GSG Workbook, which is available as a free downloadable PDF from my website: www.amyowilliams.com.au

🐞 - Wherever you see this ladybug image, this denotes you can find this particular template in the Workbook.

THE GRIEF SURVIVAL GUIDE

Contents

Chapter 1: Wrapped Up In Guilt	171
Chapter 2: Strategies For Coping With Guilt	175
Chapter 3: Grief And The Emotional Layers	181
Chapter 4: Triggers	187
Chapter 5: Healing	191
Chapter 6: How To Manage Grief	195
Chapter 7: Practical And Proactive Things To Do	205
Chapter 8: The Important Events In Life	219
Chapter 9: What To Say And What Not To Say	223
Chapter 10: Things I Wish I'd Known	229
Chapter 11: Meditation: Inner Peace	233

CHAPTER 1

Wrapped Up In Guilt

Guilt. One of the strongest emotions grieving people have.

After Joe died, I started feeling guilty literally hours after: *"Why wasn't I there? I should've known. Could I have saved him?" Why didn't I get him to go to the doctors?"* and then later, years down the track: *"Why didn't I see that he was stressed? Why didn't I do anything about his sleep problems?"*

Joe died of Focal Coronary Arteriosclerosis, in other words, heart failure. There was absolutely nothing that could have been done. Even, if I was with him at the exact time AND had a defibrillator machine, he still probably wouldn't have survived.

Arteriosclerosis is the build-up of fats, cholesterol and other substances in and on the artery walls, causing obstruction of blood flow.

Joe did NOT have high cholesterol, nor high blood pressure. He surfed, he ran, he cycled. He was always active. So, how does someone so young, fit and healthy die of heart failure?

It will always remain unknown. What actually caused the fatty build-up, the doctors cannot answer.

I believe that stress was a big contributor to his death.

This brings further amounts of guilt. I could've helped him lower his stress levels. I could have, should have, would have... Done anything.

But I have had to learn to be okay with this. To be okay that it was not my fault. That there really was nothing I could've done to prevent Joe from dying.

One reason why we experience guilt and blame is that our brain wants order and control. Although when we are grieving, we often fail to see this connection. Without someone or something to blame, we have to accept that the universe has caused this upheaval, and there may be no rational reason why this has happened.

When we hold on to guilt, we believe we could have controlled the outcome. Perception of control is often more comforting than considering we have no control.

Guilt is a low-vibration emotion, and it is a complete waste of our time and energy, serving zero purpose.

We were not born with guilt. It is an emotion we have learned over time by observing our environment we were bought up in. Guilt is something we *feel bad* about because we either did - or didn't - do something we believe is right or wrong.

More often than not, it is another person's perception they are projecting onto you. It may not align with *their* values, thoughts or opinions. Sadly, we then take this on as our own and are left to deal with it, to pick up the pieces, and made to *feel bad*.

The Grief Survival Guide

When it comes to grief, sadly those that are the closest to you, i.e. family, generally make you feel the most amount of guilt.

You are constantly *feeling bad* because of whatever someone did or didn't want from you, you either did or didn't do according to *their* needs, opinions or thoughts.

When guilt strikes, ask yourself:

"Is this their issue, not mine?"

"Is this a perception they are projecting onto me?"

"What are my values, thoughts and opinion about this situation/event?"

No one can actually *make* us feel guilty. We do it all by ourselves. And one reason is we have taken on someone else's view or comment as our own, and we believe it to be right or wrong.

CHAPTER 2
Strategies For Coping With Guilt

Below are 6 strategies for coping with guilt. I like to call the first 3 steps:

The A.M.Y Ritual.

<u>A</u>ccept. <u>M</u>editate. <u>Y</u>?

1. Accept

First and most importantly, you *must* accept and acknowledge that you feel guilty; even if you believe you *are* guilty or could have changed an outcome. Acknowledgement is power. Your thoughts create your words. Your words create your emotions. Your emotions create the low or high vibrations you live in.

The more you say and acknowledge the guilt, the more the feeling will lessen. You give the emotion less power.

Say and write down: *"I accept and acknowledge that I feel guilt towards......
I forgive myself. I will create space to accept and acknowledge that I
could not have changed the outcome."*

2. Meditate

Meditation has been a life-changer for me. Meditation or stillness has become one of the most significant mental health strategies for coping with all sorts of life experiences.

To create space to just *be*. There is a plethora of ways to meditate or learn how to meditate. Everyone is different with how best they like to do this.

For me, if I want to create stillness and calmness to let any messages come through, I much prefer to be in nature, ideally the beach or the hills; with just the pure nature sounds, a quiet place with no one else around, and my journal. I tune in to the sounds around me and just sit and listen. If any thoughts or to-do lists come into my mind, I gently imagine myself flicking them away, high into the sky.

I like to listen to meditation music on *Youtube*, too. My favourite is by *Spirit Tribe Awakening; in particular the 528Hz Positive Energy/Miracle Healing Frequency*. You can also try out many meditation apps like *Head Space*, *Smiling Mind*, and *Insight Timer* until you find the right one for you.

3. Why?

Journal and ask yourself why:

WHY do I feel guilty?

Why am I saying this to myself?

Am I taking on someone else's guilt? Why?

The Grief Survival Guide

Does this serve me any positive purpose?

Was there anything I could have done to change the outcome?

Your brain needs order. Once you have answered your questions on paper, your brain can then file these away, so the thoughts don't end up on a continuous loop.

4. Stay Positive

Positive thoughts can balance out negative guilt thoughts. Sometimes, it's hard to catch ourselves in the middle of thinking a negative thought. We go on through our entire day having so many negative thoughts, but we often don't stop and consider them.

Even if you can't catch yourself in the moment (although that is the best way), at the end of the day, try to think back and remember as many of those negative thoughts around guilt you may have had. Write them down and then next to them, write a positive spin on that thought. For example:

Negative thought: *"I should have been there when Joe died."*

Positive thought: *"I was so lucky to have spent so many amazing moments with Joe."*

You can take it even further and write a short story:

"I was so lucky to have spent so many amazing moments with Joe. I especially loved the time we spent in our van, drinking cheap French red wine, and eating baguettes with ham and cheese. It was so funny when we had to drag out the port-a-loo. I remember we cracked up laughing for so long."

The aim is to replace the small little guilty digs you give yourself, to these beautiful, loving memories that *matter* so much more. Put these positive and loving memories up on your fridge, pantry or mirror. Anywhere where you can visually see them.

- Go an extra step further and create a mood board for guilt. Create this either with printed photos, magazines and writing or digitally on *Pinterest*. Arrange the photos of your loving memories, along with your positive thoughts onto a *PowerPoint* page or a canvas board. I discuss more about this in **Chapter 7 – Practical And Proactive Things To Do.**

- Talk, talk, talk. It's essential to keep talking. Talk to anyone that will listen. And go as far as recording a voice memo if no one is around at the time when you need to get these emotions off your chest. Talk to a friend, a counsellor, a Psychologist, or a holistic counsellor. Friends and family are free... Use your resources.

- Forgiveness. By forgiving yourself, it doesn't mean you forget, condone or excuse what has happened, but it does mean you find a way to positively move forward.

5. Write An Apology Letter

Firstly, to your deceased spouse/partner/friend. Tell them all the things you are sorry for. Continuously write, don't worry about spelling or grammar – it can be hard to do! But absolutely necessary, as otherwise, it stops your free writing.

Secondly, write an apology letter to yourself; yes, from yourself. Tell yourself why you don't need to be sorry. Tell yourself how absolutely amazing you have been throughout this process. Tell yourself how much your spouse/partner/friend loved you and that you deserve freedom from this emotion that is entirely pointless and purposeless.

As one of my favourite quotes says:

"If it's out of your hands, it deserves freedom from your mind too."
(Ivan Nuru)

6. Be Your Own BFF

Think about what your best friend might say to you.

Imagine you are your own best friend. Hug yourself and be kind to yourself. Say nice, encouraging, loving words to yourself. You deserve to feel loved, supported, acknowledged and forgiven.

CHAPTER 3

Grief And The Emotional Layers

What really helped me heal was understanding where all my emotions were stemming from. When I started peeling back the layers from *anger*, there were so many other emotions simmering underneath.

My anger started as:

"Why him? It was so unfair that HE had to die. I am so angry that he left me. For not saying anything, for not going to doctors, for not being here, for leaving me with three kids on my own."

I couldn't shake the anger. I should've been grieving and sad, but for quite some time, I was just angry. But just simmering underneath all that anger, was *hurt*.

I was so hurt that he'd left me. I was so hurt that he wasn't here to see me, and the kids live and grow. I was so hurt at all the things he would miss out on. I was hurt that all our plans ceased to be real.

Underneath my hurt, was *fear*.

I was so scared to be on my own. I was so scared of how I was going to bring up three kids on my own. I was so scared of what to do next, and how to move forward. I didn't know life without Joe. I was scared to discover *"me"* on my own.

Underneath my fear, was *despair*. How the hell am I going to do this?

My anxiety attacks were feelings of utter despair of being on my own, doing it all by myself, having no support, having no one to lean on, having no husband.

Right under despair, was my *grief*.

I was so sad. So, so sad. At times, I couldn't breathe because I was crying so much. I missed him so much.

Grief is all these emotions, and more. Understanding where our anger comes from, where our hurt and fears come from, where our despair and depression comes from... It all stems from grief.

I was able to *let go* of my anger because I had accepted and acknowledged that it was *hurt* I was feeling. Once I accepted and acknowledged my hurt, then fear, then despair, I could accept and acknowledge it was my grief that was at the inner core.

So, the big question is: *"What do you do about grief to be able to let go of that emotion?"*

I talk more about this in **Chapter 6: How To Manage Grief**

See the *Emotional Guidance Scale* (originated by Abraham Hicks):

Just knowing where your anger is actually stemming from, will ease the burden of this strong emotion and low vibration.

The Grief Survival Guide

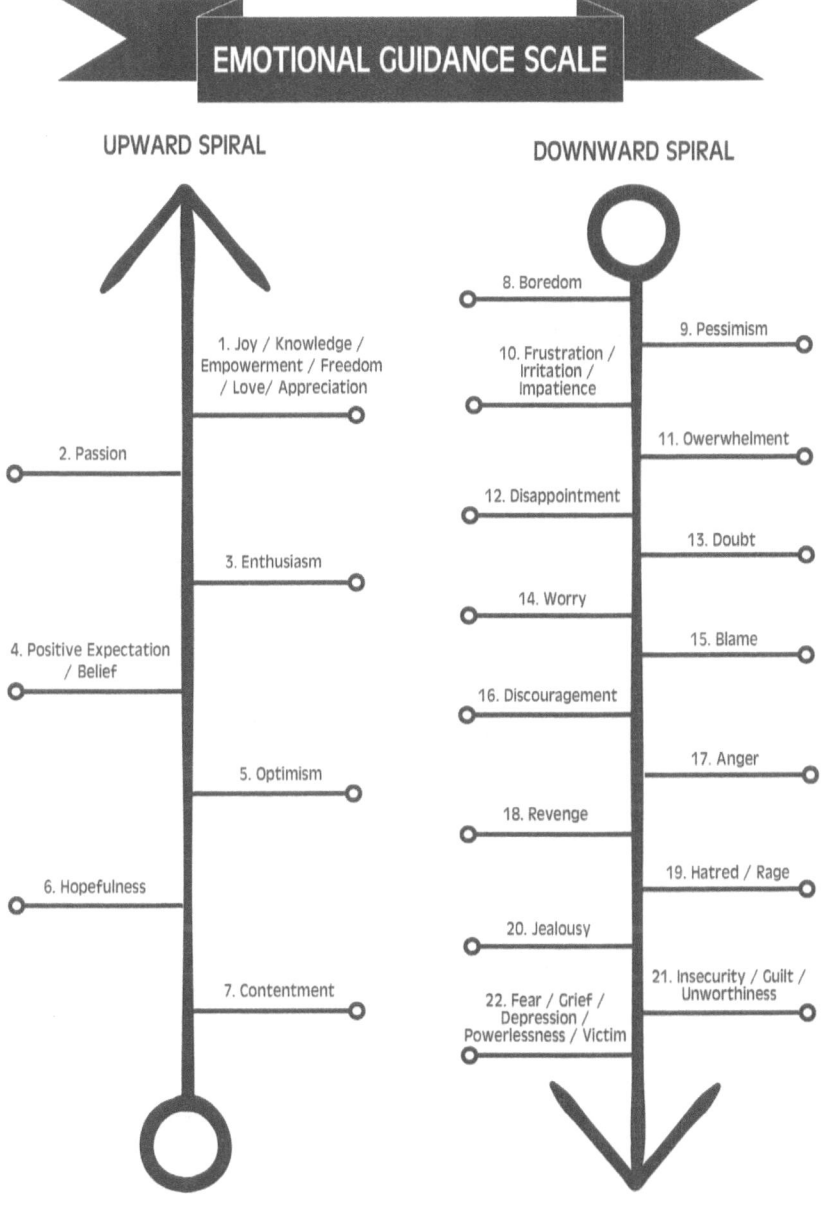

SINK or SWIM

There is nothing wrong with anger. In fact, it is getting you one step closer to a higher vibration, rather than staying in guilt, fear and depression.

When you start feeling any low vibration emotion, from boredom and blame to anger and guilt, just know, all these emotions are stemming from GRIEF.

Always remember, grief is LOVE - just at the other end of the spectrum. You are grieving because something or someone, so meaningful and valuable to you, has been taken away from you. You *will* go through many different emotions. You *will* go through these in a rollercoaster form. You just need to make peace with the fact that not one size fits all. There is no simple step-by-step guide, and out you come, good as new.

You may experience several different emotions all in one day, from deep sadness to anger to frustration to impatience to disappointment, back to sadness again.

There are no rules, there is no *right way* to navigate grief.

Ride the waves, let them come in and out. Some days those waves will be huge and scary, crashing on the shore, taking everything out in its path. Other days, the water will be calm and steady, like gentle summer waves slowly making their way up the embankment, before slowly retreating again.

Accept and acknowledge.

And just know, it will be okay. YOU will be okay.

How did I shift my grief into moving forward? It was all to do with HONOUR.

The first balloon I released on the first anniversary of Joe's death, I wrote:

"Always in your honour."

The Grief Survival Guide

From that moment, I knew that everything I was going to do, going forward, I would do it in honour of Joe and make him so proud of me. And, I wanted to be proud of myself. I felt intense emotions of strength and courage. I felt like he was by my side, supporting me more than ever. He knew I could do this. I knew I could do this.

My inner warrior had arrived. She was going to ride this roller coaster with me. As will your inner warrior arrive, too, just when you need them to.

CHAPTER 4

Triggers

What triggers your grief?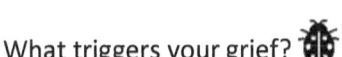

So many situations can trigger your grief, and sometimes we don't even know why we are feeling a particular emotion at the time. We don't know what the trigger is. Grief doesn't always appear as *sad* or showing tears and crying. That is why grief has so many layers. Our emotions are full of layers.

Anxiety was my biggest trigger of grief. I would have panic attacks in the car driving to a friend's house. I would wonder why the hell was I feeling this way? I was only going to a friend's house, so why should I feel so anxious about it?

Even though I didn't know why this was happening, the trigger was *the unknown*. I was not consciously thinking about anything, but subconsciously, those signals to my brain caused the flight or fight response.

Back in the day, it was like I was going into a battle, getting ready to fight, my body switched on, ready for whatever was to come.

You can also be triggered by a past situation. There could have been a time when you suffered abuse, neglect or trauma in your childhood. Even though you may not be able to draw a straight line to these moments, of what you are currently going through, your body has stored this event and is triggering you to say, *"Hey, I've felt this feeling before. I've felt unsafe, I've felt neglected, I've felt unsure."*

The only way to fully understand and be friends with your *trigger* is to acknowledge it, and by doing so, you have the power to let it go. You can't shake a feeling by not knowing what is causing that feeling.

By getting to the root, the very inner core, you need to dig deep and peel off the layers, one by one. This can take time and sometimes needs to be done with a professional.

I recommend you start with the A.M.Y. ritual and move through Steps 4 to 6. Then re-visit **Chapter 3: Grief And The Emotional Layers.** Fill in the template with your own emotional layers; try to get to the inner layer of grief.

This will be a massive *ah-ha* moment. You will see, right in front of you, how your emotions lead to grief. You might be working through disappointment as your first major emotion. Work down, and imagine you are literally peeling off the layer of disappointment and ask yourself, what is simmering underneath? Trust your instincts. Go with whatever feeling first pops up for you.

CHAPTER 5

Healing

Time does not heal all wounds.

Time may make your emotions less intense, less frequent and less of an emotional rollercoaster - but that doesn't mean you are healed.

Twenty years can go by, and if you haven't healed, you will continuously be triggered by grief emotions. There may be other events in your life that will be traumatic, or you may lose someone else. This will be a trigger and will take you straight back to your original loss and grief. Not only will you be grieving for the second time, but you will also be bringing up all the emotions you felt twenty years ago. Your grief will be two-fold.

Healing has nothing to do with time.

Healing a traumatic event is done by accepting, acknowledging, learning what your triggers are, and peeling back the layers to the inner core of your grief. It means being aware and working through all your emotions, you go through with grief. The anger, the hurt, the jealousy, the disappointment, the despair, the loss, the love.

Healing is being able to turn your grief into love.

You will always miss that person, you will always remember the memories of the traumatic event, you will always wish it never happened and that you never lost them. That is a given that cannot be taken away.

If you have hurt, if you have anger, if you have blame, if you have guilt; these must be dealt with before healing can occur.

You don't need to go alone and do this yourself. Seek professional help.

Gemma, my holistic counsellor, helped me go into the depths of my grief and peel back my layers. She helped me see so much more than what I could see. She was honest and sometimes brutally so, but I needed to hear it. She took me back to my childhood, to see my choices growing up were a condition of what my *inner child* saw and felt.

Healing is not easy. Healing is not all lovey-dovey emotions and thoughts. Healing takes courage, time and commitment. You will need to go where it hurts. That is the honest truth.

But let me ask you this. If time is going to pass anyway, would you rather do nothing and at the end of say ten years, still be consumed by grief, hurt, and all the other layers; or would you rather do the work and go to the hard places but feel happy, enjoy life, love and move forward with a lightness to your load?

It is your choice.

But I can guarantee it is worth all the hard work. It is worth going to those inner places you are avoiding and don't want to go. Because THAT is where the healing occurs.

CHAPTER 6

How To Manage Grief

1. Let It Out

As with any emotion, you need to let it out. If it stays inside, it will boil over. Believe me, I've been there many times.

It is vital in your healing process to have moments when you reminisce and go through old photos and videos (if you can manage it) of you and your loved one. Put some music on that reminds you of them. I would put on soppy love songs that I know Joe would have hated, but they made me feel and connect, and to be honest, I wanted to be sad. I wanted to let out my grief that was starting to simmer again.

I have a surfboard of Joe's that was signed by everyone at the funeral (hundreds of messages). I couldn't read that board for months, but when I did, oh boy, the flood gates opened. It was painful. It was so, so, sad. But it was healing. It was one tiny step that I couldn't take the week before.

2. Be Your Own BFF 🐞

As mentioned in the *6 Strategies For Coping With Guilt*, this can work for ANY moment you feel low, or you are hating on yourself. Imagine you are your own best friend. Think about what your best friend might say to you. Hug yourself, be kind to yourself. Say nice, encouraging, loving words to yourself.

You deserve to feel loved, supported, acknowledged and forgiven.

Fill the template with all positive words and phrases YOU as your best friend would say to you. Laminate it and pin this up on your fridge or mirror. Every time you hate on yourself, find your best friend words and write them down. Read them out to yourself every day, morning and night. Whatever it takes to shift your mindset.

Remember: *"Your thoughts create your words. Your words create your emotions. Your emotions create the low or high vibrations you live in."*

3. Express Gratitude

It is extremely hard whilst grieving to feel any sort of gratitude. The reason being is because gratitude lives in the highest vibrational frequency, alongside optimism, happiness, love and joy. It is near impossible to jump the vibrational ladder from grief to joy in one step. But, it can help you get one step closer to climbing the ladder.

Sometimes, when we are grieving, we WANT to stay in grief because we feel it is honouring the person we have lost. And the fact is, we ARE so sad and miserable without them. These exercises are not about ignoring those feelings or thoughts. We can still absolutely miss our loved ones but do so in a higher frequency vibration. We can feel joy and love and at the same time, miss our loved ones. We can miss them and love them with precisely the same intensity. But we are doing so out of love, rather than grief.

Beware, this is when GUILT will often rear its ugly head! We then feel guilty for feeling joy and love. This is when you must return to the *6 Strategies For Coping With Guilt.*

Loving what you have is an excellent way to start daily gratitude. Every day, morning or night, write in your journal - or on a sticky note or your phone - three things that you are grateful for what you have right now. Eventually, you will find you can make a much longer list than just three!

It helps shift your mindset into the positive vibrations, lifting you out of a deep dark place. Maybe not straight away, but practising these small techniques every day, will get you into a positive mindset, where you can feel happiness, joy and freedom.

Freedom from those heavy emotions that take up so much more energy and effort, where you can feel lighter every day.

Think of your body, mind and soul collectively as being either a feather or a big heavy rock. It would be much easier floating around like a feather, rather than dragging ourselves around, full of heavy rocks.

Feathers = high vibrations – our positivity, our optimism, our joy, our laughter and love.

Rocks = low vibrations – our guilt, our shame, our depression, our grief.

4. Be Your Own Fairy

This may sound a little *"woo-woo!"* but it's not! When we live in the high vibrations of energy, the outer world can see and feel it. You often hear the phrase: *"He had a great energy and vibe about him."* This is the energy we feel. And in turn, it makes us feel good, too!

When we lift other people up, we actually are lifting ourselves up, as well. It feels so good when we help someone else out. We feel good about ourselves. Think about all the natural disasters that happen and the collective communities that come together to help each other. The pride, the joy, the sense of comradery.

That's all high-frequency energy that is attracting like for like.

You can be your own fairy by spreading joy, smiles, and laughs onto others. Start small with a meaningful *"Hello, how are you?"* to the checkout person, or your local barista. Or *"Hey, I love your jacket/hair/jewellery!"* to someone passing you by. It feels good to receive a compliment but even better when you give them.

You can make a difference to someone else's day - or week - just by connecting, giving out a compliment, and just generally being nice!

You never know what someone else is going through. This was a HUGE revelation for me in the early days of losing Joe.

I would be out shopping for new clothes for the kids. And I would stop in my tracks and wonder why the hell I was shopping, and my husband was dead. I looked at people around me and had a realisation of knowing they had no idea that I was now a widow with three, young children to care for. They had no idea how much I was hurting and suffering. And they weren't meant to.

Everyone has their own story. Everyone has their own grief, trauma or loss at some point in their lives, sometimes even without knowing.

When you are grieving, by spreading a bit of joy, and being your own fairy, it helps lift you up. Even if it's the smallest amount, it will do wonders to your emotional state.

Before you know it (it could be years later) you have developed a self-taught skill of spreading joy onto others. You will be the one that others will be saying what good energy you have. You will feel lighter, you will feel happier, and you will feel more in control of your emotions and feelings.

5. Have A Purpose And Get Excited

Even in the early days of my loss, I needed a purpose. I felt lost if I didn't have anything to focus on - apart from the obviousness of grief, kids, life, etc.

I needed a purpose for ME.

Something that I could do outside all of my other have-to-do and needs.

Interior decorating was my outlet and highly therapeutic. It was the first time I felt my body, mind and soul was somewhere else, other than grieving. It was a huge relief to feel some sort of freedom in my mind.

Having a purpose, no matter how small or big gives you direction and a different focus.

Your purpose could be a daily activity, or a weekly function to attend, or a 12-month plan of studying or learning a new hobby or sport.

Put it in your planner or diary as one of your to-do tasks. This will be a task just for you. It will give you some direction and focus on something fun, something you look forward to doing, something that is therapeutic to you.

Swimming was very therapeutic to me, as well. I would often once a week head to the local pool and do laps. It was so freeing and calming, and I was oxygenating my body as well, giving me a boost and making me feel good on the inside.

Find your little bit of purpose and excitement amongst your grief.

You deserve it.

I never knew that the simple act of painting a room would lead me into a better direction for my life.

You might start running, see where it leads you.

You might start writing a book, see where it leads you.

You might have always wanted to learn to cook, do a class and see where it leads you.

Find a purpose, small or large, short term or long term. If anything, it gives you something else to focus on. Something else that is totally FOR YOU.

6. Discover Your Legacy

It occurred to me that I had a LOT of amazing things to say about Joe in my eulogy.

Not only was Joe a man of integrity, honour and strength, but he was loved by everyone who met him or came into contact with him. *He* had that energy about him, a vibe, an aura that I wanted to be around.

He was an inspiration to his mates. He was motivating and full of life. He connected so well with everyone around him, whilst always being true to himself. He had a sparkle in his eye, a gorgeous and infectious laugh and smile. The gravitational pull I felt towards him was something I have never felt before or again.

How do you want to be remembered?

What do you think people would say about you in their eulogy?

Do you want to change this?

What type of role model are you for your children? What do they see in you, that you want to see in them when they grow up and have their own family?

Reflecting on these questions can really help you dig deep into the core of yourself.

Be open and honest with yourself. You may love who you are! You may not need to change anything. But the more you recognise what you think other people see in you, the more you can focus on your strengths and weaknesses.

Be brave and write your own story! What an amazing legacy to leave.

7. Set Healthy Boundaries

I've really only recently learned and discovered healthy boundaries. And boy, do I wish I knew more about those in the early days.

Everyone wants to come and see you and have a cuppa tea or a chat and see how you are doing. The problem with that, is sometimes it's because *they* want to talk, they need to get things off their chest, or they want to find out more.

Sadly, sometimes it's actually not for your benefit. Learning to say 'no' will protect your energy.

During my first week without Joe, someone bought over bags of supplies, from kids' snacks to a full pantry load of goodies and useful items. I feel terrible (not guilty!), but I can't remember who that was. But I was extremely grateful for the love and support they showed me and the fact being it wasn't about them, it was about me. They didn't need to follow up and make sure I was happy with the supplies or ask any further questions. They just bought what they felt was necessary, for the kids and I.

My family were around 24/7, so my friends knew I was being looked after. Joe's mates would pop in, and we would laugh and cry together, listen to music, and share loads of banter about Joe. They all lifted my spirits, and I absolutely loved and appreciated all the help and support I received.

Setting healthy boundaries when you are grieving is vital for your own wellbeing, growth and healing.

Help is amazing and always appreciated. But it can be draining. You need to cater to other people, when you may not feel like it. You need to produce some energy to give to the conversation when you may not feel like it.

12 Ways to Set Healthy Boundaries:

1. Say "No, thank you." if you really don't feel up to it. Ask them to please check in again the next day as you may feel differently.
2. Put a new message on your phone stating if you don't answer, to please leave a message (either text or voice) and you will respond when you can.
3. Give time limits on visits.
4. If someone is going to pop over, ask them to bring you or them something to eat or drink.
5. If you have chores to do, don't let them stop you. Tell them you have washing, ironing and dishes to do, so can they please help while they are visiting.
6. You may feel like having company but not necessarily wanting to talk. Ask them to help you with some gardening or tidying up the yard or taking the dog for a walk.
7. Be honest in telling them where your head is at or how you're feeling.
8. Be open about what you do and don't want to talk about.
9. Your friends and family would be relieved to know if you want them to just talk about what's going on in their life. It can be a nice distraction for you.
10. Ask them to take you out if you've been stuck at home. Visits don't always need to happen in your environment.
11. Tell your friends and family what you need from them. Your support network will want to help as much as possible. Put yourself in their shoes, and you would want to do the same.
12. Remember, they are not mind-readers, they really don't know what you need or want. Perhaps you don't either, but as time goes on, you will start to feel what is more beneficial to you, what you really want from your support, and what you don't want.

8. Build A Growth Mindset

Building a growth mindset and suffering from grief, really don't go hand in hand. This is more to do with YOU; your mind, body, and soul. It's about how you feel on the inside, about how to help yourself feel lighter, so you are not consumed by the heaviness of grief.

To have a growth mindset through grieving is to take tiny steps every day or every week, to climb up into the high-frequency emotions.

Making time for yourself is extremely important and necessary. This is the time to be selfish.

Ask Yourself:

How can I nurture myself today? How will you take care of *you*?

What three things can I do for myself this week?

What small step can I take to raise my energy vibration?

My time out was spent mainly at the beach, walking along the coast, sitting at Joe's plaque at Trigg Beach. I would take myself clothes shopping, go get massages, have a float in the pods, take a bath at home. I would include music, candles, essential oils, crystals, burning sage and Palo Santos, wherever I could.

All of these soothed and nurtured my mind, body and soul. I looked forward to my next bath ritual or my next massage booking. These small rituals I did for myself, raised my energy, sometimes only slightly, but I would feel lighter, and I would definitely feel calmer and more relaxed. I would feel that I could function and take on whatever was coming at me next with the kids or on my to-do list.

This is your growth. This is where your mind, body and soul can let go, have some peace and invite in some beautiful vibes, messages or pure stillness.

CHAPTER 7

Practical And Proactive Things To Do

1. Creating Routines And Diary Management 🐞

The most helpful and practical advice I was given by a counsellor, was to create a routine for myself, the kids and my support network.

I didn't realise the importance of organisation and diary management until the first few weeks of having family over, and us all feeling very lost and not knowing what to do and how to do it.

Not only does that save you from a million questions all day, every day, but it gives your support network a practical and easy to follow routine that makes them feel they are contributing the best they can.

Your support network will know exactly who is helping and when.

Have someone close to you to help you set this up – usually a parent, caregiver, friend, or family member. Choose this one person to be your *'Personal Assistant'*.

SINK or SWIM

At this point, everyone will want to do something to help. You are not a burden. You must for your own health and wellbeing accept this help. Let people help! They WANT to because they know they can't fix your pain. They can't fix your deep grief. They don't know what else to do apart from help.

This main person will be the new *you* for as long as it takes. They will take over and take care of all the little things, so you can focus on you, your wellbeing and most probably all the taxing phone calls and letters to deal with regarding the death of your loved one.

Taking on the burden of your deceased loved one's affairs is hard enough, without needing to do all the other jobs you do in a day.

If you don't have any family around you, choose a friend, or a colleague. Someone will WANT to help. Or nowadays, using our online presence, all these steps can be done via *Zoom* and online. Contact can also be made through social media platforms.

In the *GSG Workbook*, I have created a *Schedule Planner* template that you can print out and fill in.

Here is an example:

Task/Activity/Appointment: Take kids to school	When: Monday, Tuesday, Wednesday, Thursday and Friday	Who: Sarah Mary
Task/Activity/Appointment: Put bins out	When: Monday nights	Who: Adam
Task/Activity/Appointment: Clean the pool	When: Every Friday	Who: Pool Cleaners Josh Phone No.

The Grief Survival Guide

HOT TIPS:

- Laminate the Schedule Planner so you can easily change dates, and who is doing what job. Or, alternatively, use a whiteboard or a blackboard and pin-up in the kitchen for everyone to view easily.
- Schedule and highlight your own time out!
- You can change the template to be a Food Planner, so your support network knows what dishes you like or don't like. There's nothing like getting ten dishes of tuna mornay if you don't like it!
- You can also add to the Food Planner what meals your kids will eat, what they have on their sandwiches, what food to keep in-stock in the pantry, and the kids' special snacks and treats they like to eat or drink.
- Create a *Whatsapp* or *Facebook Messenger* group chat, so all your support network can collaborate, and everyone knows what is happening.
- Give your phone to your closest helper so they can answer and screen your calls.

2. Therapy And Counselling

Find what works for YOU.

There is no rush! I went straight into traditional talk therapy, first with a grief counsellor, then a grief Psychologist, and I suffered terrible anxiety.

It was way too raw, too soon, too real.

This is what worked for me:

Taking time out at my favourite place to be.

Find your place. Somewhere quiet, where no one will interrupt or bother you. Somewhere in nature; the beach, a sundeck, a boat, a jetty, a comfy chair in your house, or the local pools tend to have areas with deck chairs. Somewhere you feel comfortable, relaxed, at ease, and most importantly, safe.

There's nothing worse than getting somewhere to relax, and all the other elements don't make it that way. By that I mean, the sun, the wind, people, hunger, thirst, etc.

HOT TIP: Get yourself a bag that is always packed ready for your time out.

I didn't like to travel too far, so I went to my local beach. In my ready-to-go bag, I would take a beach umbrella, a comfy beach chair, my music (phone), ear pods, a journal, a pen, a jumper, my lip balm (never went anywhere without it!), hat, sunglasses, water, protein bar snacks, tissues, a beach towel and, of course, a bikini.

I would lay down, close my eyes and just start by listening to sounds around me. This helped me to quiet myself. Taking deep breaths, in and out, listening to the sounds. If thoughts came into my mind, I would imagine flicking them away up into the sky where they disappeared.

This was my sacred time.

This was where nothing else mattered except me. That's right. It's your turn to be selfish. There are no problems you need to solve right now. There's nothing you need to fix. Your children are fine. Your family is fine. This time is all about you.

Different types of counselling or therapy are very personal, depending on how you resonate with them.

My first two grief counsellors were traditional talk therapists. In the early stages, I found it wasn't helpful for me. I soon realised I was a practical person and needed practical to do help, not just talk about my loss and my feelings over and over again.

After about eight months or so, a school mum and friend referred me to Gemma, a holistic counsellor. Immediately she resonated with me.

She too had lost her husband, so she knew first-hand what grief was like, specifically losing a husband.

Adam Hansen, a good friend of mine and Joe's, offered to help me with my trauma using NLP. I was suffering from colossal anxiety and wanted to get more to the root of it.

NLP stands for Neuro-Linguistic Programming. He used a technique called *Memory Resolution,* sometimes also known as the *Eye Scramble technique.*

I had no idea that one of my triggers and the main cause was around the day Joe died.

The vision of seeing Joe on the floor, the colour of his skin, the gurgling of blood I could hear when giving him CPR, the blood trickling out of his nose, his locked jaw, the sound of the kids crying while I was trying to speak with the paramedics over the phone, and knowing they were just standing there watching the whole scene unfold.

The NLP was amazing and completely stopped my visions of the scene of Joe on that day. It's not to say it cured my anxiety, but it certainly was a huge layer that I was able to peel off.

Now when I picture the scene, the image just drops out of my head. I can't visualise it. I can talk about the day Joe died now without having a body and mind collision of anxiety. I can state the facts and keep the emotions and feelings very separate.

I would highly recommend trying a wide range of therapies available, as you never know which one will totally transform your grief, and it will really help you move forward positively.

3. Spiritual Guidance

Spiritual guidance can be whatever it needs to be for you. For some, that includes the likes of meditation, crystals, and oracle cards. For others, it may be creating stillness within to perhaps hear any intuitive messages you may receive.

Spiritual guidance for me was by far the most helpful and resourceful focus. I eventually gravitated towards meditation, exploring crystals that I was drawn to, and buying several different oracle card decks. I absolutely love connecting using these methods, and I can really feel my intuition take over. I feel in flow and expansion every time I create space and time for these rituals.

Firstly, however, seven years ago, I knew of no such thing! I thought it was all *hippie stuff* that wouldn't actually help me.

After seeing Gemma on and off for many years, I attracted several other people into my life on their own spiritual journeys.

I saw a lady named Antonia, who lives in Perth. She doesn't like to be called a healer, but she is. She was born with a gift and talent and uses that to service other people. She helped me go deeper within myself and really find out who was there.

This was where she said she could see my wounded warrior woman.

She was beaten up, exhausted, and so badly needed a rest to recuperate. I could see myself wounded inside. I could see the image of my wounded self, leaning up against a tree, with scars, blood, and absolute defeat written on my face.

I needed to look after me. I couldn't keep going on being wounded.

I faced my layers of guilt and fear.

The guilt of not working a traditional 9-5 job.

The guilt of not always interacting with my children.

The guilt of spending too much money on *'unnecessary'* things that I believed I was being judged on.

The guilt of having too much me-time.

Fear of being judged!

Fear of not always doing the right thing.

This guilt and fear still live inside me, but I am friends with them now. I know when those feelings come up, that I have been triggered and that I need to accept and acknowledge that is how I am feeling.

Meditation, for me, is a beautiful place. I can go and infuse my mind, body and soul with calm, quiet and peace. It's where I go to recharge, to heal and to gain more strength so I can keep on going in life.

There is nothing to lose by giving some *"woo-woo!"* a try! You may even find yourself there.

I saw a Medium, named Cliff Rollins, about eight months after Joe passed. It's not for everyone, but I can almost guarantee anyone who has lost someone very special to them, will do just about anything to feel close to them again.

I can say it was an amazing experience that filled my heart with love, joy and tears. It was all so worth it. It's crazy, and sometimes, unbelievable. But until you go and experience it, you won't know the effect it has.

4. Journaling

Journaling or writing in a diary can be one of the best methods of expressing what is going on inside yourself. It doesn't have to be neat. It doesn't need to have the right spelling or grammar. Just write, and you will soon be spilling out entire conversations, feelings, thoughts, as all that inside dialogue comes out. As they say, better out than in.

I kept a journal for over a year, and it is very insightful reading back my thoughts and what was happening for me at the time. I wished I had kept it going for longer.

The reason why I didn't is that I felt like sometimes journaling would feel like a big task or something that needs a lot of energy and brainpower. I really didn't have much to give, even putting pen to paper.

Later on, many years down the track, when I was looking at studying meditation, I came across an extremely helpful tip for journaling. It was a list of 'feeling' words.

The idea is you scan over the words and pinpoint how you are feeling inside and write those down. I found it extremely helpful, firstly, by actually confirming what I was feeling, and secondly, it put my feelings into words, and thirdly, I could read and write down those words and make more sense of why I was feeling that way. Then the journaling flowed so much easier, and I found it not to be a chore, but rather an exploraton of myself. And, even explore further as to why I was feeling that way.

In the GSG Workbook, I have created a 'Feeling Words' template that you can print out and use with journaling.

5. Mood Boards

I first started exploring mood boards when I was studying my Interior Design Diploma. It was such a creative outlet and fun exercise that I started doing them for all sorts of things!

Mood boards can be an extremely powerful and therapeutic exercise. They help get out what is in your head and plan and organise the chaos into a beautiful story and memory.

You can create as many mood boards as many times as you feel the need to. You may like to have a mood board for each emotion you struggle with. You can keep adding to it, capturing why this emotion has come up, or how it has made you feel. Only you see this, so you don't need to explain anything. Words, affirmations, quotes, memories and photos say a thousand words.

There are several options for creating mood boards. You can use PowerPoint or search online for apps for digital ones. I like to stick with the simplest and most creative form of cutting and pasting.

Just this exercise alone is very therapeutic.

You can print out photos of your loved one and cut out inspirational words, or perhaps cut out feeling words. Or even write them on the mood board. You can go to a craft store and get stickers to stick on, like stars or emojis, maybe a cloud for feeling low and moody, or a sun for feeling happy and bright. You can buy the old-fashioned stamp and ink pad and bash it down on the paper getting some frustration out.

6. Time Out

For me, this needed to happen often. I am so lucky to have amazing parents and in-laws that help out very regularly. But in turn, they get to have the most uniquely special bond with their grandchildren.

Having time out whilst you are grieving is so, SO important. I can't state this enough.

Whatever time out looks like for you, is different to everyone.

My time out included going to the beach to just lay there, going for walks, visiting friends and going out and being social – plus the pub! I needed my life, too. I needed to look after my needs, and not just as a mum. I needed to look after Amy's needs as a whole.

Think about what you are really yearning to do, or is there something you wished you had the time to do but kids or family stopped that?

It is time to be selfish. You need this.

Time out can be as small as having a cup of tea outside in the sunshine for 20 mins with no distractions… Ahhh, absolute bliss.

Time out can also be as long as booking a retreat, hotel, or holiday away somewhere for days or weeks if you can.

Time out can be whatever you want it to be, because it is for YOU, and you only.

7. Discover New Loves

For the first part of losing Joe, I hung on to what we did together. We travelled, we went on road trips, he surfed, and I watched. Wherever I went, we had been before. Memories were everywhere, and at first, it was triggering me and was very hard to face. Being around other surfers, hearing the sound of their leg rope hitting the board, the smell of the wax, all of these were like a slap in the face; it was extremely painful.

Until I started to make my own new loves. I still wanted what we had. It was like wanting something so badly but realising it was never going to happen. I had to let go of those loves we had together and make new ones.

Now, I love self-discovery, mindfulness, meditation, crystals and all that! I love Yin Yoga, Pilates, venturing out to the hills for a bushwalk, swimming, going to the beach with no expectations or time limits or boundaries. I love listening to new and different music. I love how much time I spend with my family now. It has got to the point where previously; Joe's lifestyle would not fit into mine anymore.

I've missed out on our planned Australia trip with Joe and our little family, but I've made other memories. I've taken the kids camping down to Margaret River, a three-hour drive on my own. I've also driven us 1200km to Coral Bay with my family.

I've just had to learn that there are many new things I can explore and do with just myself and my kids.

8. Get Out In Nature, Explore And Move

The most magical things happen when we are out in nature, exploring and being in the moment. It grounds us and makes us appreciate what is right in front of us.

Nature offers us beauty and strength, calm and peace, wonder and enchantment.

Try and find a reserve or somewhere in your area that has trail walks. You'll probably find a lot of dog walkers there, and that itself, being with animals can be uplifting.

Either gather some friends; or do it on your own.

I love nothing more than wandering peacefully through the forest or on the beach on my own. You can just be you. Let out your emotions. If no one is around, scream into the woods, or out to the ocean. It can feel so liberating.

Being out in nature also moves your body. Going for walks or any amount of exercise gets the blood pumping through your body; it releases endorphins to give you a natural high. It boosts your energy levels and makes you feel lighter, calmer and relaxed.

Your brain has time to un-frazzle. You can make more sense of things and perhaps, let go of some built-up negative emotions.

Try doing some meditation whilst in nature. Stop, breathe, listen, and breathe some more.

I would imagine Joe next to me, either just sitting there or having his arm around me. It would really comfort me. It took away all the other shit that was running through my head. All I would do is feel him, I would feel his breathing, I would feel his chest and arms around me.

I would choose to make this moment an uplifting, encouraging and loving moment, rather than sad and lonely.

9. Join Facebook Pages And Reach Out To The Community

All I wanted to do in the early days was to find other widows that had lost their husbands. I only wanted to connect with those that would know exactly what I was going through.

In 2013, there were no *Facebook Pages* or community groups to join. I remember talking with my mum about it, and we were just so shocked that nothing existed to help grieving widows. Indeed, there were quite a few of us out there, but the lack of support groups was a massive blow for me.

I felt so alone in my journey for so many years.

My mum even looked into starting up a group herself, just to provide me with the support and help I was yearning for from other widows.

To be able to join forces with others going through the same pain connects you to a community that gets you.

You don't have to be fake, you don't have to put on a smiley happy face, you can vent to people that don't know you, and in return, you receive support, compassion, understanding, forgiveness and lots of virtual hugs!

CHAPTER 8

The Important Events In Life

There are going to be many notable and important events that come up that you will have to adjust to.

No Christmases, Birthdays, Mother's Days, Fathers' Days, or Anniversaries will ever be the same again.

Even though they will not be the same, you can make them new. Everyone is different, and every situation is unique, that not all rituals will fit and feel right with you.

The most important thing is to *accept and acknowledge* how different it will be.

The more you try to make it the same and perhaps avoid dealing with the absence, the more intense that absence will feel.

Firstly, have a good think and have an idea about how YOU want the new way to look and feel. Everyone will have their own opinion, so you should plan in your head how you feel you would like the celebration to be done.

Next, ask your family and friends or whoever is relevant to the celebration what YOUR ideas are and how they feel about it. It is always worth getting close family members opinions and thoughts as it can help structure and add things in to help the celebration. Plus, they feel they also get to be involved in how the day or event will look and feel.

The new way doesn't have to be set in stone. The following year you may feel it didn't quite work and change it. So, try not to be too concerned with it being the forever ritual. One year you may not feel like changing it or celebrating the event, and that's okay, too.

Try to have a focus on positive and uplifting changes:

How do you want to *feel* that day?

How do you want to *honour* your loved one?

How do you think your loved one would like to *see you* on that special day?

If you do or don't change a celebration out of spite, you will only end up having a miserable day yourself. If there is too much tension with family members or friends, I would suggest no celebration be made, or everyone does it their own way, and that the following one may be the right time to celebrate with newfound love and honour.

CHAPTER 9

What To Say And What Not To Say

One of the hardest times for me was going into Henry's school to drop him off. I felt like I was an alien, and everyone was staring at me.

I knew everyone knew.

I knew they didn't know what to say to me. How to act. I had all these conflicting feelings and thoughts about who I was meant to be and how to be that person. I didn't want to give off any wrong impression. What if I smiled? Did that mean I wasn't showing my grief?

I felt less pressure being around strangers. They didn't know. I could be whoever I needed to be at the time. I would sit down at the beach and bawl my eyes out, and clearly, be heard. But I didn't care. I could also sit and smile and not feel like I'm sending out the wrong message.

I don't know why I felt so concerned with how I looked or how I came across. I guess I was worried about being thought of as not grieving anymore. People are so quick to judge on outside appearances.

It is well known that the most depressed and vulnerable people are those, who on the outside, give no signs of showing just how deeply troubled and miserable they are.

I would often get told, *"I'm here for you. Just let me know what I can do."*

That is not overly helpful for a grieving person. It may make the other person feel good about themselves because they've offered help, but this now puts more pressure and decision making onto the grieving person. They now have to think about, *what can this person do for me? What help do they mean? Can they cook? Can they be here at night-time to help with the kids? What time can they be here during the day?* Instead, the grieving person will continue as they were, regardless of the offer to help.

The griever cannot deal with any more decisions then what they have to. Their world has just been turned upside down. They do not even know what they want to eat for lunch. Let alone think about how someone can help them and then make an effort to call them and organise it. That is just asking too much of them. Instead of asking a question, state a fact to offer precisely what you WILL do for them (not just *can* do for them).

For example:

"I am here for you. I will come over this evening at 6pm and will help you get the kids to bed."

VS

"I am here for you. Let me know what you need."

You can see the difference in how helpful the first statement is vs the second question.

The Grief Survival Guide

🐞 *A grieving person needs to hear you recognise, understand and acknowledge their pain first, before making statements of strength and moving on.*

The below table is an extremely helpful guide to give to any of your support people:

What not to say to a grieving person	How the comment is received from the grieving person	What and how to say instead
I can help you if you like?	I have no idea what capacity of help you can provide. I really can't think of what I can get you to do as there are so many things I need help with.	I will help you with _____ (this).
I am here for you.	In what way? What can you actually do for me?	I will support you by doing _____.(this) for you.
When can I come see you?	I have no idea how I'm feeling from hour to hour, let alone day to day. I don't know.	I will drop in on _____ (day) at around _____ (time). If you are not home, it's not a problem. I will arrange another day with you later.
Anything you need, you let me know.	I don't know what your capacity is of what you can help with. Now I have to think of what job you can do for me.	I am a landscaper. I will come over on _____ (day) at _____ (time) and tidy up your yard.

Let me know when you need some time to yourself and I can look after the kids.	I don't know when that will be. Does that mean you're willing to come over at 8pm at night?	I understand you will want some time to yourself. How about I come over on __ (day) at _____ (time)? I will take the kids out for 2 hours.
It will get easier as time goes on.	No, it won't.	You are doing the best you can right now.
It's good to see you moving on.	Moving on? I will never 'move on' from grief or love or my loss. I may move forward, though.	I understand this journey has been incredibly hard for you and is still continuing, but I do admire your positive mindset in what you are achieving at the moment.
I don't know how you do it.	I would love to run away from this, but I have responsibilities that I must and have to do.	I can only imagine how extremely hard it must be, to do all that you are doing, whilst grieving.
I wouldn't be able to cope like you.	Yes, you would, because you would HAVE to.	I can only hope that I would have your same strength and mindset if this happened to me.
You seem so strong.	Why, because I'm not constantly crying? Because I'm not curled up in a corner, rocking? Because you don't see me lose it?	It must be so exhausting having to get on with life when you've had no choice to. But I see you are an amazing positive person that is doing the absolute best you can.

CHAPTER 10
Things I Wish I'd Known

1. You don't have to answer the phone or the door! If you don't feel like talking, then don't.

Put a note on your front door to let others know you are okay but need some alone time. Put a message on your phone saying:

"Thanks for checking in. If I don't answer, please leave me a message or text me, and I will return your call when I can."

2. You are not alone.

Seriously. I used to think I was the only one up at 2am, 3am, and 5am breastfeeding my baby, but of course, I wasn't the only one. It's the same as grief and loss. There are so many people going through such deep sorrow, hurt, anger and pain.

HOT TIP: Reach out to your FaceBook community pages. Post a message to say you are a widow/widower and would like to know if anyone else in the area would like to catch up for a coffee and talk. Even if you get one person. That one person can be the best support and help you need.

3. Phrases such as, *"It will get easier. Time heals all wounds. It's time to move on."* - get used to hearing these all the time. People who have not been through your grief will not know what to say. They do not mean to say the wrong thing. It is society's fault for not dealing with grief very well.

4. No one talks about grief. No one knows HOW to talk about grief. We weren't bought up talking about grief or sadness, or many other emotions really.

5. Ride the waves. Sometimes you have good days, the water is calm and just flows nicely. Other days it's wet and wild, and the waves crash on the shore with such ferocity that you are back to being stuck in your deep hole.

6. If you have kids, the most heartbreaking times are thinking of them without their mum or dad. All the events you go to, you go alone. You see all the other kids' parents with two parents. It breaks your heart that they don't have both their parents and you don't have your spouse/partner with you to join in with the celebrations. That missing hole will always be there. At those times, it feels deeper and hollower than ever.

7. Kids and grief. One of the best pieces of information I was told early on was that kids are lucky in that their brains are not fully formed until late teens or around 21 years of age. They don't have the ability to forward think and plan. They live in the moment. They live for today. Try not to carry their grief as well as your own.

8. For now, just focus on yourself and today, the present moment. The future, even the following week, is not known.

9. You will start to receive mail addressed *"To the estate of your husband/wife..."* This can be a trigger.

10. Promised help will disappear. People will get on with their own lives. This is only natural and is not to be taken personally.

11. We shouldn't have to ask for help. But, in reality, we do. Three to four months in, the daily drop-ins or check-up calls and messages are a lot less frequent.

12. DO ask for help though, because our friends and family ARE standing by.

13. I wish I had let go some of my *"I will just do it myself"* attitude and sent a message out for help. I wish I had just made the phone call to someone, instead of feeling like no-one was there to help.

CHAPTER 11

Meditation: Inner Peace

This guided meditation is to help those with very active minds who find it difficult to 'not think' during quiet times.

It is aimed to give your thinking mind a break, whilst using your body to feel emotions, thoughts and feelings.

This meditation includes visualising. With visualising, go with the first image that comes up. This may come to you as a word, a picture, a feeling, a colour or a shape. Whatever the 'image' is, just trust that this is your meditation, your way, your vision, your messages.

If you don't know how you feel or what you see. Just take a moment in that space and ask yourself:

"How do I feel in this space?"

Take some mindful breaths. There is no rush to see or feel something. Just trust that you are being guided to where to you need to be. Your subconscious is taking it all in, even if you feel you are not 'receiving messages' or you doubt yourself and think you are not really in a meditative space because you can still feel your brain thinking.

Come back to your breath, be in your space of where you are. That is all you need to do.

I recommend you record yourself reading this meditation first, then play it back and listen.

You can record on your iPhone using 'Voice Memo' or a similar tool for Android phones. Talk slowly and softly for the best effect.

Let's begin.

Sit in a comfortable position.

Close your eyes.

We are going to relax and calm our minds and body by firstly doing a breathing technique.

The sequence is:

Breathe in (for 4 counts) through your nose
Hold (for 4)
Breathe out (for 6)
Hold (for 4)

When you breathe in, imagine you are sucking in white wispy clouds. They find their way all-around your body, from the tip of your head, slowly moving down to the tips of your toes.

When you breathe out, imagine the clouds are magnetic and have picked up all the negative energy inside your body, turning the white clouds into grey.

Blow out this grey matter through your mouth, as if you are blowing out a candle. Send it on its way.

The Grief Survival Guide

Repeat this three times. Try to breathe deeper and longer each time.

If you feel like you still have some excess energy that needs clearing, gently shake your arms and legs and feel the excess energy leave from your fingertips and toes. Send it on its way.

Breathe normal and stay in this space.

I want you to imagine you are sitting on a couch.

Imagine your couch; however, you would like.

What colour is it?

How does the fabric feel?

How are you positioned?

What is the size of the couch?

Take a moment in this space, and just FEEL all your surroundings.

Now, imagine the room you are in. Have a look around you.

What does the room look like?

What is the feeling of the room? Perhaps it's warm and cosy? Perhaps it's cool and calm?

Take a moment in this space and just FEEL all your surroundings.

Now, imagine a TV screen is in front of you. You have the remote in your hand, and as you turn it on, a vivid white light appears on the screen.

As you look closer at the white screen, you notice the white space is filled with white fluffy clouds. They are moving ever so slowly like on a light summer breezy day.

SINK or SWIM

You stand up and walk towards the screen. You reach out to touch the screen, and your arm disappears into the whiteness. You can feel your arm in the empty space behind the cloud.

How does it feel on the other side?

Can you FEEL what the space may look like?

You then step your whole body into the white space through the TV screen. As you enter, you know you are entering a new world. You feel a buzz of light around you.

Have a look around you.

Where are you?

Look down at your feet on the ground.

Take a moment in this space and just FEEL all your surroundings.

Take a few mindful breaths.

Breath in this new air.

Let it in through your entire body.

This air is so fresh and clean. It feels as though you are on top of an arctic mountain. So pure.

You see a path in front of you. You start walking along this path.

What do you see?

How do you feel?

Take a moment in this space and just FEEL all your surroundings.

The Grief Survival Guide

Is there a particular powerful emotion coming up?

Check in with your heart, and ask, what do you feel?

Whatever it is, trust it and just be with the emotion.

In silence, the soul speaks.

With the first word or feeling that comes to you, answer the following:

I AM feeling...

I WILL find the courage to...

I WILL release...

I AM thankful for...

Take some mindful breaths.

Now, see yourself walking back along the path. In front of you, you see a swirl of white light where you entered this world.

You reach out and touch the white light. It is time to come back. You step into the light and find yourself sitting back on your couch.

Just sit quietly in this space for a moment, knowing your soul has spoken to you.

When you are ready, open your eyes.

Journal any insights, feelings, or thoughts that came up for you.

Notes

www.ingramcontent.com/pod-product-compliance
Lightning Source LLC
Chambersburg PA
CBHW021833110526
R18278200001B/R182782PG44588CBX00012B/19